Remembering S R Nathan

A MENTOR FOR ALL SEASONS

Mushahid Ali • Kumar Ramakrishna

S. Rajaratnam School of International Studies,
Nanyang Technological University, Singapore

World Scientific

NEW JERSEY • LONDON • SINGAPORE • BEIJING • SHANGHAI • HONG KONG • TAIPEI • CHENNAI • TOKYO

Published by

World Scientific Publishing Co. Pte. Ltd.

5 Toh Tuck Link, Singapore 596224

USA office: 27 Warren Street, Suite 401-402, Hackensack, NJ 07601

UK office: 57 Shelton Street, Covent Garden, London WC2H 9HE

Library of Congress Cataloging-in-Publication Data
Names: Nathan, S. R., 1924–2016, honouree. | Mushahid Ali, editor. | Ramakrishna, Kumar, editor.
Title: Remembering S.R. Nathan : a mentor for all seasons / [edited by]
    Mushahid Ali and Kumar Ramakrishna.
Description: New Jersey : World Scientific, [2017] | Includes bibliographical references.
Identifiers: LCCN 2017010484| ISBN 9789813222809 (hardcover) |
    ISBN 9789813222816 (pbk.).
Subjects: LCSH: Nathan, S. R., 1924–2016. | Presidents--Singapore--Biography. |
    Singapore--Politics and government.
Classification: LCC DS610.73.N37 R46 2017 | DDC 959.57/052092 [B] --dc23
LC record available at https://lccn.loc.gov/2017010484

British Library Cataloguing-in-Publication Data
A catalogue record for this book is available from the British Library.

Copyright © 2018 by S. Rajaratnam School of International Studies

All rights reserved.

Desk Editor: Karimah Samsudin

Picture courtesy of the Nathan family.

Contents

Message by K Shanmugam — xv
Foreword by Eddie Teo — xvii
Preface by Ong Keng Yong — xxiii
Acknowledgements — xxix

Introduction — 1
A Mentor for All Seasons — 1
Mushahid Ali and Kumar Ramakrishna

REMEMBRANCES — 9

    Eulogy by Lee Hsien Loong — 11

    Eulogy by Vivian Balakrishnan — 18

    Tribute by Mary Liew and Chan Chun Sing — 23

    MFA's Tribute to Mr S R Nathan — 26

    Eulogy by Tommy Koh — 29

    A True Friend — 33
    Zainul A Rasheed

    Lifelong Mentor and Friend — 37
    S Chandra Das

VIEWS FROM ABROAD — 43

The Unassuming Statesman — 45
C Uday Bhaskar

In Memoriam: President S R Nathan, A Friend of Indonesia — 48
Jusuf Wanandi

S R Nathan: A Friend in Deed — 52
Kalimullah Hassan

S R Nathan's Academic World — 62
Paul Evans

CONDOLENCE MESSAGES FROM SOUTHEAST ASIA — 67

Negara Brunei Darussalam — 69

Kingdom of Cambodia — 70

Republic of Indonesia — 71

Lao People's Democratic Republic — 72

Malaysia — 73

Republic of the Union of Myanmar — 74

Republic of the Philippines — 75

Kingdom of Thailand — 76

Socialist Republic of Vietnam — 78

PICTURES

REFLECTIONS: FOREIGN SERVICE 79

The MFA Years 81
Barry Desker

Boss, Mentor, and Friend 91
Calvin Eu Mun Hoo

Calm and Cool Leader 96
A Selvarajah

S R Nathan: Mentor with Heart 100
Seetoh Hoy Cheng

S R Nathan: The Thought Leader 108
S Gopinath Pillai

REFLECTIONS: SECURITY AND INTELLIGENCE 115

S R Nathan and His Leadership Role
in the Laju Affair 1974 117
Tee Tua Ba

REFLECTIONS: SOCIAL SERVICE AND COMMUNITY BUILDING 137

S R Nathan and His Social Service Legacy 139
Jennie Chua

Lessons I Learnt from Five Decades of Interaction
with the Late Mr S R Nathan 145
K Kesavapany

A People's President Who Inspired Singaporeans
to Build a Better World   155
Jean Tan

REFLECTIONS: LABOUR AND TRADE UNIONS   161

Union Befriender, Media Rescuer   163
Peter H L Lim

Stabilising Industrial Relations   177
Tan Ming Hui and Stephanie Neubronner

REFLECTIONS: MEDIA   183

Diplomat, Media Boss, and President   185
Yang Razali Kassim

Bridging Media and Government: S R Nathan's
Unique Role   192
Han Fook Kwang

REFLECTIONS: RESEARCH AND ACADEMIA   199

A Man For All Seasons   201
Kumar Ramakrishna

S R Nathan and the Institute of Defence and
Strategic Studies (IDSS): The Formative Years   207
Ang Cheng Guan

Nurturing a New Generation of Scholars   213
*Joseph C Y Liow, Bernard Loo
and Bhubhindar Singh*

APPENDICES   219

1. Testimonial Letter from Miss Jean M Robertson, Senior Lecturer, University of Malaya, 1955   221

2. Citation for the Conferment of Fellow of the Singapore Association of Social Workers to Mr S R Nathan by Associate Professor Ann Wee, 2008   225

3. Citation for the Honorary Degree of Doctor of Letters by the Public Orator, Professor Bertil Andersson, President, Nanyang Technological University, 6 December 2011   231

4. Speech by Mr S R Nathan Director, Institute of Defence and Strategic Studies at the Inauguration Ceremony, 1996   236

List of Abbreviations   239

References   243

Remembering S R Nathan: A Mentor for All Seasons

Message

K Shanmugam

Mr S R Nathan's life story tells us of an individual who has left us a remarkable legacy and to whom Singaporeans owe a debt of gratitude.

Many of us know Mr S R Nathan as a statesman and leader. He responded to the call of duty in fields such as social service, labour, intelligence and diplomacy. He led the Security and Intelligence Division, Ministry of Foreign Affairs and, later on, served for two terms in the highest office of the land. He dedicated his life to serve fellow Singaporeans, exemplifying professionalism and excellence.

The chapters of this book reveal yet another aspect of Mr Nathan's life story — that of a colleague, mentor and friend. The writers share their personal interactions and encounters with Mr Nathan. They give us a rare glimpse into how Mr Nathan cared deeply about people and touched the lives of those around him.

I encourage you to read these chapters and learn more about Mr Nathan's life story. I trust that this life story will continue to inspire future generations of Singaporeans.

Mr S R Nathan, patron of the Inter-Religious Organisation, with Mr Shanmugam and members of the IRO celebrating Mr Nathan's birthday in June 2014. Picture courtesy of Imam Syed Hassan Al Attas of Ba'Alwie Mosque.

Mr K Shanmugam *is Singapore's Minister for Home Affairs and Minister for Law.*

Foreword
Remembering S R Nathan

Eddie Teo

I count it a blessing and my good fortune to have had the opportunity to work under Mr S R Nathan in the early part of my career in the Public Service. He was my mentor, guru, and boss when we were in the Ministry of Defence. He was one of the most savvy and street-smart persons I have ever met. Even though he lacked formal academic qualifications, he was extremely intelligent and shrewd, and very knowledgeable and well-read. He had superior political instincts, and a deep understanding and sensitive feel for the history and culture of our region and its people. His foreign counterparts from the West, in particular, were always keen to tap him for insights into what was happening in Southeast Asia.

He had a very high EQ and could get on with people from every strata of society. He had many friends, and he never forgot them. He has personally helped so many people, and so many of us owe so much to him. He has given his whole life to public service. In a note he dropped me after we had lunch three days before his recent stroke, he referred to "the purpose we all shared in our lifetime". Obviously, serving the nation had given him true meaning and purpose in life, on par with his devotion to, and love for, his family.

I never figured out where he got these attributes and how he honed his survival instincts until I read his memoirs. He learned to survive through the incredible hardships he faced when he grew up. He developed tremendous resilience and true grit by overcoming the misfortune and hard knocks he suffered in life. This also explains why he sounded so incredulous when he spoke about starting from such humble beginnings and ending his career holding the highest office in the land.

Like other members of our founding generation of political leaders, Mr Nathan lived a very simple, frugal, and unostentatious life. For the whole period I have known him in our 40 over years of friendship, he had always lived in the same modest house in Ceylon Road. He used to have us over for Deepavali there, but moved the annual party to the Eurasian Club across the road when his guest list expanded and he could no longer accommodate his friends and colleagues in his humble home.

He earned the trust of our founding political masters because of his unwavering loyalty and his proven capability. Lee Kuan Yew, Dr Goh Keng Swee and S. Rajaratnam all turned to him for advice, and entrusted him with the most sensitive and difficult jobs in government because they knew he was very capable and absolutely dependable. Mr Nathan never refused them, and always fulfilled his duty diligently and with total dedication.

Being loyal is not the same as being a 'yes man', agreeing with everything the politicians say. Mr Nathan was very discreet about the period in the Ministry of Defence when we worked closely together. Aware of the need not to compromise security, he has never publicly revealed anything sensitive we did there and said very little in his memoirs about his work. But he has written about his relationship with his Minister, Dr Goh Keng Swee. His account revealed how he was not afraid to stand up to the great man and defend his own people when he thought that Dr Goh had made a wrong judgement about certain individuals. If you knew Dr Goh, you would know that it took great courage for someone to disagree with him. Mr Nathan did, and Dr Goh eventually came round to change his opinion of the officers he had initially condemned. Mr Nathan's explanation was that sometimes, our political masters needed time to cool down, and they would then regret their initial impulsive decisions to sack those they thought were wanting.

Mr Nathan was a demanding boss and a hard taskmaster. He expected his officers to work as hard as he did, but he was also a caring and nurturing boss. Over the years, he became a good friend, and someone I respected and could turn to for counsel and advice. Every year, without fail, he never forgot to send a basket of flowers to my house for Chinese New Year. His stupendous memory meant he could remember names very well, and would always ask about my wife by name. He also kept in touch with many of his foreign friends, some of whom would seek him out when they visited Singapore, or never failed to ask about his well-being.

When he was President, Mr Nathan would occasionally invite me to have a quiet and private lunch with him in the Istana, and we would speak freely with each other about the challenges we faced, and share our perceptions of what was happening in and outside Singapore. Before the lunch, he would ask me what I would like to eat, and I would always suggest hawker food (which I knew he liked) such as *mee goreng* or chicken rice, and he would immediately agree. I hope Mrs Nathan will forgive me, because I know she was very strict about his diet at home.

Although Mr Nathan has written several books on his life, he has kept the choicest morsels of his personal anecdotes for his friends. I will always remember the stories he told me of his experiences working with our founding fathers in post-Separation Singapore. He related one such anecdote when I saw him in hospital last year, after he had his first stroke. Even though the event occurred 50 years ago, in telling the story, S R could remember the details with fantastic clarity, as if it had happened only the day before. Anyone reading his memoirs will realise how remarkable a memory he had. This ability to recall details and facts made him a fascinating raconteur in social settings. His friends will surely miss his company in future gatherings.

In recent years, Mr Nathan has felt obliged to share his experiences with younger Singaporeans, and kept busy meeting them in small groups for private chats. Just the other day, when I learned that a scholarship candidate had interviewed Mr Nathan for a school history project, I asked her what she thought of him as a person. She said she found him engaging, and he was very generous with his time, taking the effort to offer her good advice on many things. She concluded by saying she thought that, like Wee Kim Wee, Mr Nathan was truly a 'People's President'. I trust the people of Singapore, especially those who have met him, will share this young Singaporean's assessment of the remarkable man.

On my part, I will miss him dearly.

Mr Eddie Teo *is the Chairman of the RSIS Board of Governors and also the Chairman of the Public Service Commission. Mr Teo retired from the Singapore Public Service in 2005 after a 35-year career and worked with Mr S R Nathan at the Ministry of Defence.*

Preface
Man of Guts, Instinct, and Tenacity

Ong Keng Yong

I first met Mr S R Nathan soon after I joined the Ministry of Foreign Affairs (MFA) in June 1979. His reputation was awesome. He came to MFA as First Permanent Secretary a few months before I entered the Foreign Service. When I moved around the Ministry corridors at City Hall then, the talk was all on how Mr Nathan shook up MFA. He introduced a full-time MFA duty office and the 'morning prayers' — the daily meetings of heads or deputy heads, where they would brief him on issues of significance. He invented the 'Information Notes', and these were produced a few times weekly to keep the Cabinet members and other top officials informed of what was happening in foreign affairs and their implications for Singapore. The policy briefs were jazzed up, and maps were included as annexes. He rejected 'palavers' — long-winded narratives or woolly recommendations — in MFA submissions. Many MFA staff members on posting abroad were scheming hard to extend their overseas assignments by hook or by crook!

S R Nathan's 'Praetorian Guard'

My seniors in MFA, however, told me that Mr Nathan would shower 'love' on the 1979 batch! It was the first time MFA could recruit 11 officers in one calendar year. Therefore, they thought that Mr Nathan would develop this 'bumper crop' into his best 'Praetorian Guard' for the Ministry. Sure enough, Mr Nathan paid a lot of personal attention to us from the 1979 batch.

Mr Nathan soon instituted an area specialisation Master's studies programme for the 1979 batch — we would be sent out in groups of two or three over time to be trained as Arabic, Indonesian, Thai, Vietnamese, and other ethnic speakers, with a strong grounding in history, politics, and society of the countries concerned.

I went to Georgetown University in Washington, DC for two years. Mr Nathan disagreed with then Prime Minister Lee Kuan Yew when he sent me to Washington, DC for Arab Studies. Mr Lee believed that Cairo was the place that MFA officers should go to learn about the Arabs and their language. Mr Nathan, on the other hand, supported the view that Georgetown University and the US capital city would be a better venue for MFA to train its professionals in the nitty gritty of the Arab world, and to understand the big power politics inflicting harm and impinging on the future of the Middle East countries.

The Coin and Other Lessons

Before I went to do my Master's degree, I learnt several things from Mr Nathan. Two points were ingrained in me. First, no job is too big or too small. Second, there are two sides to everything. He believed that all MFA officers must be able to do the strategic thinking and writing, as well as the administrative and operational chores. An Ambassador of Singapore must go through all levels of diplomatic work and to be able to manage a team of Foreign Service Officers in any of our embassies abroad.

Occasionally, Mr Nathan would act like he was the Chief of Protocol, and double-checked all the physical arrangements for the visits of our political leaders overseas and incoming visits by foreign dignitaries. He institutionalised many standard operating procedures (SOPs) to ensure that all preparations and contingencies are within anticipation and control.

Mr Nathan would show me a coin on a few occasions. He said: "There are always two sides of the coin." He would stress that, as civil servants, we must never outshine the political office holders in the open. At the same time, we must not take all the things they say as a royal decree. The important thing is to talk about the different angles of any issue and come to a sensible decision. There must be an awareness of the extreme positions one can get from trying to tackle any issue.

For Mr Nathan, the political office holders must be engaged in a polite and strategic manner as they were elected to public office and are responsible to the people, while civil servants chose to be the professionals in public service. He advised me that the differences must not be mixed up. "Civil servants are not the political leadership and we have different tasks and responsibilities", he would often point out to me. Mr Nathan left me with this profound technique — whisper the right note at the right time to the right person to get the desired results.

Time for Simpler Things

I served as 'Number 2' to Mr Nathan in our embassies in Kuala Lumpur and Washington, DC. His diplomatic skills and energy level left me panting for breath very often. Still, he had time for simpler things. For example, we were required to sing after office hours with then High Commissioner Nathan and Mrs Nathan in the embassy multi-purpose hall as a group every week for two months.

The reason was that he discovered MFA staff in KL did not sing our national anthem "Majulah Singapura" well enough. The boss paid for a professional music teacher to polish up our rendition of the national anthem. Along the way, we were taught to sing beautifully Frank Sinatra's "My Way", and another song about tying a yellow ribbon around the old oak tree. These lessons enabled me to have at least three songs for the karaoke gathering at the end of various official meetings in ASEAN circles.

The humble man in Mr Nathan always championed the chap from the 'normal stream'. He would give one chance, then another chance, and even a third chance for his subordinates to measure up. He saw good in almost every person he worked with. Even those he criticised and scolded occasionally, he would forgive them, and shower care and love. I feel that Mr Nathan believed that the most useful asset of a person is not a head full of knowledge but a heart full of love with ears open to listen and hands willing to help.

Man of Guts, Instinct, and Tenacity

Mr Nathan told me to visit smaller colleges and less prominent universities in America where Singaporeans were schooling. That brought me to places like Iowa, Minnesota, Nebraska, and Oklahoma. His main concern was to demonstrate our embassy's care of Singaporeans beyond the Ivy League and blue-chip institutions of tertiary learning. Through this kind of networking, Mr Nathan helped our embassy in Washington, DC reach out to many people in far-flung places. Many Singaporeans saw him as an Ambassador who was earthy, practical, and one who had time for the ordinary man. Mr Nathan made a difference in many people's lives. He captured the imagination of Singaporeans young and old.

I would like to read you what our former Chief of Protocol, Chin Hock Seng, said of Mr Nathan:

> Mr Nathan was a man who made his mark on our country, its institutions and its officers. He left both a professional and personal imprint on me, as on many others. A wider understanding of my work, my attitude and outlook springing from that, my desire to do justice to the job, and will to overcome obstacles to get it done — so much of it all was transmitted to me over time by exposure to Mr Nathan's character and values. The two and a half decades of my public service career and my work life today, is marked by habits formed and shaped while serving Mr Nathan in different capacities.

I fully agree with Chin Hock Seng. Mr Nathan has left a deep imprint on my own career and my life.

I can go on much more on what Mr Nathan had done for MFA and Singapore. The fact is this is a humble ordinary man who became a super achiever with his guts, instincts, and tenacity. He was so natural. However, he continuously drew on each episode of his fascinating life to be a better person and an extraordinary leader of our community. For me, Mr Nathan is the grand 'Jedi' of the special class of Singapore warriors, protecting our society from the dark side, to borrow an analogy from the Hollywood blockbuster movie series "Star Wars".

I was fortunate to be at the bedside of Mr Nathan at the hospital before sunset on the day of his passing. He was unconscious and breathing heavily, even though his blood pressure had stabilised. After a few moments with him, I leaned forward and said: "Have a good rest, Sir."

This tough yet kind man had worked relentlessly his whole life for a country he helped to build. I salute him. He is a legend for our nation and will always be treasured.

Ambassador Ong Keng Yong is the Executive Deputy Chairman at the S. Rajaratnam School of International Studies. Ambassador Ong previously worked with Mr S R Nathan at the Ministry of Foreign Affairs.

Acknowledgements

We are grateful to all those who have contributed their Condolence Messages, Tributes, and Remembrances of the late Mr S R Nathan for the book.

Minister K Shanmugam for his Message; Mr Nathan's family for pictures of Mr Nathan; the Ministry of Foreign Affairs for permission to reproduce copies of Condolence messages from Southeast Asian leaders; the National Archives of Singapore (NAS) for permission to reproduce pictures of Mr Nathan from the various ministries; Singapore Press Holdings for permission to reproduce pictures of Mr Nathan from *The Straits Times* archives; the Inter-Religious Organisation for the picture of Mr Nathan with its members; Mr S Chandra Das, Mr Eddie Teo, Mr Peter Lim Heng Loong, Imam Syed Hassan Al Attas of Ba'Alwie Mosque and the Singapore International Foundation, for their pictures; Mr Winson Chua for the illustration of Mr Nathan on the cover; Ms Tan Ming Hui, Ms Stephanie Neubronner, and Mr Adrian Tan, for their efficient sub-editing and compiling of the manuscript; Mr Ho Chi Tim for his research assistance; Mr Richard Oon for his graphic design work; as well as Ms Karimah Samsudin of World Scientific Publishing, for her calm and professional oversight of the entire process of production.

Last but not least, we would like to thank Ambassador Ong Keng Yong, Executive Deputy Chairman of RSIS, for the initial idea of and strong support for the entire project from start to finish.

We hope this volume will, in a small way, help Singaporeans of all ages and backgrounds cherish the memory of Mr S R Nathan — the People's President, and mentor for all seasons.

Mushahid Ali

Kumar Ramakrishna

July 2017

Introduction
A Mentor for All Seasons

Mushahid Ali and Kumar Ramakrishna

He was not born great but achieved greatness in the service of his country. He had a rudimentary education but became a self-taught mentor of unionists and workers. He rose through the ranks to attain the highest level in the civil service in Singapore, in diplomacy and foreign relations, and became the Chief of intelligence and security in the defence ministry. After serving as Ambassador to Malaysia and the United States, he set up a strategic studies institute and was elected President of Singapore for two terms. Thus did S R Nathan join the pantheon of Singapore's founding fathers as a mentor for all seasons. It is no exaggeration to assert that he played his part in defining post-independence Singapore.

S R Nathan could be a mentor for all seasons because his own background was so richly textured and multi-layered. Before he scaled the heights later in life, he fully experienced the hard knocks of life in the valley, so to speak. He was born in humble circumstances, and raised in even more distressed conditions without a home and proper schooling. He had little to look forward to in life after having to leave school, and eking out a living as a hawker assistant and errand boy, sleeping in a temple in Muar. Undaunted, he got a job as a messenger in Johor Bahru, and later became a clerk in the Public Works Department and passed second in the state exams for clerical officers. While working as an accounts and personnel clerk in the Johor State Secretariat, S R continued his self-study, went to the School of Commerce in Singapore, and passed the London Chamber of Commerce exams with distinction. He studied privately through a correspondence course and obtained the Cambridge School Certificate with a Grade II in late 1951. He qualified for admission to a Diploma in Social Service course at the then University of Malaya, and obtained a Shell bursary for two years. He graduated in 1954 with a Diploma in Social Service, with distinction, and gained a job as a Medical Social Worker in the Singapore Medical Service. He was appointed Seamen's Welfare Officer in the Marine Department's Seamen's Welfare Board (SWB) in 1956, where he served for six years. His work performance gained him accolades from his Supervisor, and he was nominated as member of the Singapore delegation to an international conference in Munich (*see* Appendix 1). S R Nathan thus epitomised what it meant to work one's way up through the ranks, displaying great grit and determination to succeed in life.

When Singapore attained self-government, then Finance Minister Dr Goh Keng Swee assigned Nathan to the newly-formed Labour Research Unit to help the unions belonging to the still-to-be formed NTUC. Nathan had gained valuable experience in working with the Johor

Civil Service Association, helping in negotiations for better pay and working conditions.

Nathan found himself in the role of mentor to the trade unionists in the Amalgamated Union of Public Employees (AUPE). He also represented Singapore at the conference of the Afro-Asian Peoples' Solidarity Organisation in Algiers in 1964, and later in organising the AAPSO conference held in Singapore. That proved to be his training ground for his subsequent job as Director, Political in the newly established Ministry of Foreign Affairs in 1966. There, he not only helped Minister S. Rajaratnam in running the ministry, but also headed the secretariat that conducted the first Commonwealth Heads of Government Meeting outside London in 1971. He proved to be a competent organiser and supervisor of the young officers in the fledgling MFA, based on the principle of having a clear idea of the mission set by the political masters and dedication to do what was necessary to carry out the mission. The officers he mentored went on to become Directors and Heads of Mission abroad.

In 1971, Dr Goh asked Nathan to report to the Ministry of Interior and Defence as Director, Security and Intelligence Division (SID). Dr Goh personally brought him around to meet the departmental heads to register his endorsement of the appointment. He was to serve in SID for the next eight years, and made his mark as the government security adviser while nurturing a new generation of younger officers to support him. He also served as Permanent Secretary for Home Affairs, and in early 1974, led the high-powered team that escorted the hijackers of the Shell ferry boat Laju to Kuwait in exchange for their freedom. Thus did Nathan become a Soldier of Singapore against international terrorists. The details of this landmark episode have been well retold in the volume by former Commissioner of Police Tee Tua Ba.

When Nathan reached retirement age (55) in 1979, he was asked by Prime Minister Lee Kuan Yew to go to MFA as First Permanent Secretary with the mission to hammer it into shape. He was given two years to turn it into a first-class foreign service, failing which the PM would dissolve the Ministry and make it part of the PMO. Nathan came to MFA when it was grappling with two momentous issues — the Vietnamese invasion of Cambodia in December 1978 and China's border incursion into Vietnam in February 1979. He marshalled MFA's resources to turn it into a policy-making and action-oriented outfit to drive Singapore's foreign policy and promote its regional security. He trained young officers to take the initiative in formulating policy and leading Singapore's diplomatic forays abroad, thereby turning MFA into a first-class service.

Having fulfilled his mission, Nathan was tasked by PM Lee to take on the English language media, particularly to turn the Straits Times Press into a viable and vibrant newspaper. There, again, he assumed the role of mentor rather than monitor, and helped raise the standard of the newspaper as a reliable platform for information and opinion rather than a mouthpiece of the government. After six years of guiding the newspaper publishers and editors, Nathan was asked to change roles again — this time as High Commissioner to Malaysia, to help ease the uneasy relations and troubling issues between the two countries. Two years into the job, Nathan found himself being named as part of the problem because he was getting too close to the states and people on the ground. He was then transferred to Washington where he served with distinction as Ambassador to the United States. His major achievement was establishing Singapore as a small but stout-hearted country that stood up for its rights and sovereignty, while being a reliable friend and partner of the strongest power in the world.

However, instead of a well-deserved retirement on his return from Washington, Nathan found himself tasked by Deputy Prime Minister Tony Tan with the assignment of setting up a research institute and graduate school to provide intellectual support to the Ministry of Defence, in studying developments and devising ideas to improve Singapore's security and strategic capabilities, emulating the many think tanks and research establishments in the United States. Taking up the challenge, Nathan set about setting up the Institute of Defence and Strategic Studies (IDSS) in 1996, with the help of scholars from the United Kingdom and the United States, and building a core of local researchers to take over from them. That modest institute went on to become a graduate school of international renown, the S. Rajaratnam School of International Studies (RSIS).

Three years later, Nathan was called upon to stand for election as President of Singapore. Once more he rose to the challenge, and was nominated by the unions he had mentored in his younger days; he was returned unopposed not once, but twice, serving as President of the Republic for 12 years. He travelled extensively as a 'Super Ambassador' for Singapore, and indeed attained greatness as the 'People's President' who had given his life to the service of his nation. As one could tell from the easy rapport he enjoyed with masses of Singaporeans at the annual National Day celebrations or at the Istana, he was greatly adored by Singaporeans from all walks of life. This was no act either, as he genuinely possessed a people's touch. No doubt his early life struggles must have bestowed him a deep empathy for his fellow man that never left him.

To sum up, caring for the poor and destitute was his guiding principle, looking after the subordinates his usual practice, social service his basic training, which he applied to his various occupations and situations. He led with both head and heart — by no means an easy balance to strike.

Several former colleagues in MFA have recounted their experiences of his leadership and mentorship. While his role in MINDEF, particularly SID, is 'classified', his leading role in settling the Laju hijack is well documented, as related in this volume. He has also mentioned his role in getting training facilities for SAF in neighbouring countries. His motto has been helping others to help the nation.

He performed the role in his key appointments in SWB, LRU, MFA, SID, MHA, and MINDEF. Mr Nathan also played an advisory role as Director or Chairman of Jurong shipyards, and most notably The Straits Times Press, now known as the SPH newspaper group.

A constant theme running throughout his career in the civil service was his interest in raising the quality of his staff and colleagues, for the sake of his organisation and ultimately Singapore. We invite you to peruse the diverse contributions to this volume to get a sense of the very wide breadth of the full life and long career of S R Nathan. In doing so, we are confident that you will be able to grasp just how much he was a man of the people, a mentor for all seasons — and how deeply Singaporeans are going to miss him.

Mr Mushahid Ali *is a Senior Fellow at the S. Rajaratnam School of International Studies. Mr Ali previously worked with Mr S R Nathan at the Ministry of Foreign Affairs, where he also served as an Ambassador.*

Associate Professor Kumar Ramakrishna *is the Head of Policy Studies and Coordinator of National Security Studies Programme at the S. Rajaratnam School of International Studies. Associate Professor Kumar was recruited by Mr Nathan to join the Institute of Defence and Strategic Studies in 1999 while completing his doctoral studies in London.*

Remembrances

Eulogy by Lee Hsien Loong

Eulogy by Vivian Balakrishnan

Tribute by Mary Liew and Chan Chun Sing

MFA's Tribute to Mr S R Nathan

Eulogy by Tommy Koh

A True Friend
Zainul A Rasheed

Lifelong Mentor and Friend
S Chandra Das

Eulogy by Lee Hsien Loong

Today, we are gathered to bid farewell to our former President, Mr S R Nathan. On behalf of the Government and the people of Singapore, I would like to convey our deepest condolences to Mrs Nathan and her family.

As one of the pioneer generation who lived through Singapore's most tumultuous period, Mr Nathan witnessed many of the key events that shaped our nation. He not only had a front-row seat, but was often an actor on stage. He played a significant and influential role in our nation-building.

From a most humble beginning, Mr Nathan built a unique and illustrious public service career. He served in diverse fields, from social work to trade unions to intelligence, diplomacy, journalism, academia, and finally as President. He played a leadership role in the Indian community. But he was also a President for all Singaporeans, and cared deeply about racial and religious harmony.

Quite apart from Mr Nathan's remarkable career, the central and brightest thread in his life was his love for Umi, his wife. He first set eyes on her in 1942, when she was 13 and he 18. After a courtship of 16 years, braving parental objections and a two-year separation while Umi studied in Britain, they married in 1958. Their relationship spanned an astonishing 73 years, an inspiration to us all. S R loved and honoured Umi all the days of his life. And she, in turn, was his anchor throughout his career, including the 12 years that he was President, when she supported him with grace, charm, and warmth. Mrs Nathan, thank you very much.

I have had the honour and privilege of knowing and working with Mr Nathan for over 40 years, in different capacities: first as a young SAF officer when Mr Nathan was Director of Security and Intelligence Division (SID); then as a Minister, when Mr Nathan served as a diplomat; and later, as Prime Minister, when Mr Nathan was President.

When I think of Mr Nathan, four things come to mind. First, he was a man who lived fully, seizing all that life had to offer.

Second, he never gave up, no matter what the difficulties and dangers. Nor did he indulge in self-pity or look to others for help. Instead, he faced challenges head-on with a steely resolve, and ultimately prevailed.

Third, he always did his best for Singapore, even at personal risk and sacrifice. Whatever the mission, he answered duty's call. Singapore could absolutely rely on his loyalty and dedication. Few have answered the nation's calls so faithfully and so often, and served Singapore so well.

Fourth, he had great personal integrity and commitment. It was his character, as much as his intellect, that led to his achievements in life and took him to the highest office in Singapore.

The one incident that best epitomises Mr Nathan's qualities is the Laju Incident. In 1974, four terrorists, two Japanese Red Army terrorists and two terrorists from the Popular Front for the Liberation of Palestine (PFLP), tried to blow up the Shell refinery on Pulau Bukom. They failed, and hijacked the "Laju" — a ferry boat operating between Bukom and mainland Singapore. The Government negotiated a deal with the terrorists to release their hostages in exchange for safe passage to the Middle East. Mr Nathan, then Director of SID, risked his life to lead a team of 13 officials who accompanied the terrorists to Kuwait on a Japan Airlines aircraft. The terrorists had demanded their presence to guarantee the safe passage. The Singapore officials were, in fact, hostages.

Not many of today's generation know of the Laju incident. Those who do probably do not fully appreciate the magnitude of the decision that Mr Nathan and the other 12 made. It took great physical and moral courage. In an interview near the end of his term as President, Mr Nathan was asked if he thought he would return alive. He said: "I was not sure. Because what awaited us at the other end was something uncertain."

After Mr Nathan retired from Government in 1982, Prime Minister Lee Kuan Yew asked him to be the Executive Chairman of The Straits Times Press. This was new and uncharted territory for him. Eyed suspiciously as a former government man, he was hardly welcomed with open arms by the journalists. But his sincerity won them over.

He spent six years there. In his gentle but effective manner, he helped the journalists understand our unique context as a young nation, and gave them the support and the space to run a high quality, successful newspaper.

In 1988, Mr Nathan became High Commissioner to Malaysia. He hosted me later that year, when I went up to Kuala Lumpur to speak to the Harvard Club of Malaysia. My theme was the longstanding ties between Singapore and Malaysia. On reading my draft speech, Mr Nathan shared with me his own personal example. After the war, he had served in the Public Works Department in Johor Bahru, and earned a pension. In 1988, long retired from the Malaysian Civil Service, he was still receiving RM150 a month. I used this anecdote in my speech, which helped my Malaysian audience to warm to my message of goodwill.

This was typical of Mr Nathan. He had a knack for the small but telling personal anecdote that was a warm view, and made a personal connection that illustrated a broader point. As an aside, I gather from his son, Osith, that he continued to receive this RM150 pension every month until he passed away, and would tell Osith to file the payment slips carefully away, which Osith faithfully did.

Later, Mr Nathan was posted to Washington. He was Ambassador when Singapore sentenced Michael Fay to caning for vandalism in 1994. The US media mounted an intense campaign against the caning. Singapore needed to get our point of view across. Mr Nathan went on the talk show *Larry King Live*. He was grilled, but defended our position with conviction, and persuaded quite a few Americans that what Singapore was doing was not wrong.

When Mr Nathan returned from Washington in 1996, he established the Institute of Defence and Strategic Studies (IDSS). Now called the S. Rajaratnam School of International Studies (RSIS), it has established a name for itself internationally in strategic studies, research into extremist terrorism, and the study of multiracial societies.

Mr Nathan could have retired from public service into a more placid life in academia. But duty called again. Once again, he put country before self. He stood for President in 1999, and was elected. Mr Nathan served two terms with dignity and distinction. He enjoyed meeting people. His approachable and caring manner put everyone at ease. He won the respect and affection of Singaporeans of all races and walks of life. He firmly believed in and was the epitome of multiracialism, attending events of all communities, making time for everyone, no matter who they were. When receiving foreign visitors at home, he was ever the gracious host who impressed with his knowledge of world affairs. Overseas, he represented Singapore with aplomb.

Reflecting his generous spirit, Mr Nathan started the President's Challenge to help the less fortunate. It raised more than $100 million over 12 years, reminding us that we all have a part to play in building a compassionate society.

As Prime Minister, I worked with Mr Nathan for a good seven years. We met regularly and he gave me good advice. When Singapore encountered the 2008 Global

Financial Crisis, I went to him to seek his permission to draw $5 billion from the protected reserves to fund a Resilience Package of emergency economic measures, and to back a guarantee of all bank deposits in Singapore. That guarantee called for earmarking $150 billion of these reserves. After careful consideration, he approved the Government's request. It enabled us to deal with the crisis decisively, and to emerge from it largely unscathed. Mr Nathan proved once again that he was capable of making tough decisions when the need arose.

After Mr Nathan retired as President, his age began to tell on him, but he stayed active. He was ever willing to share a lifetime of experience and wisdom with younger Singaporeans. He continued to engage and share his stories with civil servants, teachers, and school leaders, as he had done when he was President. He put considerable effort into engaging students at the Singapore Management University, where he was a Distinguished Senior Fellow. He attended events, tracked what was happening in Singapore and abroad, and kept up with old friends and their families. He was the moving spirit behind the biography of the late Mr Ho See Beng, an old comrade-in-arms from union days, which was published last year.

I kept in touch with Mr Nathan regularly. Once in a while, he would join me for lunch at the Istana. But I am afraid to report that my food pales in comparison with what he would serve me when he was President. When I came across an article that I thought would interest him, I would send it to him. He made it a point always to reply, in his beautiful hand which remained steady all his life.

In fact, he wrote to me recently, when an old friend of his asked him to pass me a message. It was a four-page note, setting out the matter, explaining the context, and offering to convey my response back to the friend. It could have passed as a staff paper. I thought how lucky he was, to be so active and focussed at 92 years old.

There are many lessons for us to learn from Mr Nathan's life. He had hoped that Singaporeans, especially young Singaporeans, would draw a key lesson from his memoirs, which is "not to give up". It is a precept that Mr Nathan lived by. He overcame extremely trying circumstances in his childhood and rose in the public service through grit, determination, and ability, guided by a deep and abiding sense of duty. He put heart and soul into every task assigned to him, including the highest office in the land. Time and again, he placed nation before self. Quietly and without fuss, he gave his best years and more, to Singapore.

It is with great sorrow today that we bid farewell to one of Singapore's greatest sons.

Mr Lee Hsien Loong *is the Prime Minister of Singapore. Prime Minister Lee was sworn in as Singapore's third Prime Minister during Mr S R Nathan's second term of Presidency. Throughout their careers in the Singapore Civil Service, Mr Lee and Mr Nathan also worked together in various other capacities. This eulogy is reproduced with permission.*

Eulogy by Vivian Balakrishnan

Our words, and I say *our* words, because I'm reflecting the sentiments of all of us gathered here today. Our words will not add or subtract from the enormous achievements of our former President, Mr S R Nathan. But I think it is only right and fitting that we are gathered here today as members of the MFA family, to reflect, remember, and to pay tribute in his memory.

Ministries of Foreign Affairs only exist if we have independence and sovereignty. And our independence and sovereignty was thrust upon us suddenly. And it was a moment and in fact a period of great uncertainty. We were vulnerable and the future looked dim.

Because of the urgency and the sensitivity of the many tasks that lay ahead of the Ministry, it was not surprising that Mr Lee Kuan Yew put some of his best men and women into the Ministry. And Mr S R Nathan himself was transferred from the union movement to MFA. He started off in 1966 as an Assistant Secretary. I think the equivalent today would be a Director. A year later he became a Deputy Secretary, and after a brief sojourn outside, he came back to the Ministry as Permanent Secretary from 1979–1982.

Mr Nathan himself reminded us of then Prime Minister Lee Kuan Yew's ultimatum. He was given two years in which to make a difference, failing which the Prime Minister intended to disband MFA, and we would become part of the Prime Minister's Office. The fact that we are still here and still a Ministry is testament to his success. In fact, today, many of the institutional practices that we take almost for granted — information notes to encourage clear and succinct thinking and writing, 'morning prayers' which I know you all still observe, and the opportunities for country officers to give briefings on significant developments to inculcate critical thinking and to enhance and sharpen communication skills. His foresight and his efforts to build up these institutional practices have paid off.

Subsequently, he was also our High Commissioner to Malaysia, then Ambassador to the United States, and then Ambassador-at-Large. Even after being elected President in 1999, he maintained a unique relationship with our Foreign Service, imbuing his presidency with a very strong foreign policy orientation. In fact, as Mr George Yeo said: "President Nathan never really left the diplomatic service."

During his 12 years as President, he raised Singapore's international profile. He made about 30 state and official visits. He led our first-ever state visits to many countries such as Japan, South Africa, Thailand, and Turkey. He maintained the close relationship not just at an institutional level, but I know he made time for regular fireside chats with young Foreign Service Officers. Mr Nathan and the other MFA pioneers had no files, no standard operating procedures, no diplomatic training, no institutional memory banks to call on. They only had their guts, their instinct, their intellect, their total devotion and commitment to Singapore. They charted a path for our young nation, consolidated our sovereignty, built our international networks, and supported our economic development.

Today, all of us and our successors travel the world, speak at forums, and participate in negotiation sessions. It is much easier today for us to carry ourselves credibly as representatives of an independent, sovereign, successful, and cohesive nation-state. But this is really due to the tremendous efforts of the pioneer generation of MFA officers. So, let us remember that we stand on the shoulders of giants, and Mr Nathan was one such towering giant.

He played a leading role in many defining chapters of our foreign policy — signing of the ASEAN Declaration, resolving the sensitive issue of foreign bases in the region, and the Vietnamese occupation of Cambodia. He successfully defended our sovereignty and promoted our interest with that special blend of 'charm and toughness', to quote Prime Minister Lee Hsien Loong. Charm and toughness — these qualities were on full display when he served as our High Commissioner to Kuala Lumpur, and subsequently as our Ambassador to Washington. You would recall that he had to deal with episodes such as the Michael Fay incident and the many bilateral issues that came up from time to time with Malaysia, including Pedra Branca. Mr Nathan handled all these incidents with quiet and effective diplomacy, defused tensions whenever possible, maintained open channels of communications, and firmly defended our interests.

In fact, I found it ironic and maybe even fitting, that yesterday when our Embassy in Jakarta opened the condolence books for signing, there was a mini protest outside our Embassy gates. I am very proud of the response of our team. They said that this is a suitable moment to recall what Mr S R Nathan had once said about the qualities needed to be a successful Foreign Service Officer — patience, calmness, modesty, empathy, and good humour. Mr Nathan himself epitomised all these and I am glad to say that it has worked and our succeeding generations of Foreign Service Officers have learnt well. I am sure Mr Nathan himself is pleased. Mr Nathan said in his memoirs that "duty to friends and family, to my fellow men, to country is paramount to my view of life and I have tried my best to live up to this ethic". Indeed, his illustrious career exemplifies an unwavering sense of duty to Singapore and to Singaporeans. Mr Nathan served Singapore faithfully, defending and promoting our interests with utmost distinction and equanimity.

On a personal note, he was a childhood friend of my late father, and he was always this larger-than-life figure at dinner conversations. This boy whom they knew in childhood and this person from a humble background, who never forgot his roots, never forgot what it was like to be looked down upon and, because of that, gave him that special empathy to look out for the most vulnerable people. He never forgot his old friends. I remember telling him once that my father would like to have tea with him and he organised a lunch. The usual photograph, autographed in his gold pen was sent to my father and to my uncle. Before I entered politics, there were two people in government whom I consulted before I made the decision, Mr Dhanabalan and Mr S R Nathan. And I can tell you that without their discreet, honest, personal advice, I would not be here. So we all individually and collectively, owe Mr Nathan and his pioneer generation a great debt. We can never repay him, but I think we can only try our best to emulate him to pay it forward for the future of Singaporeans.

Thank you, Mr Nathan. Thank you for a life well-lived, for your devotion, for being a wonderful man and a pillar of support for all of us. Thank you.

Dr Vivian Balakrishnan *is Singapore's Minister of Foreign Affairs. This eulogy is reproduced with permission.*

Tribute by Mary Liew and Chan Chun Sing

The following letter was presented to the Nathan family following the passing of Mr S R Nathan:

23 August 2016

Mdm Urmila Nandey

Dear Mrs Nathan,

We share your pain and sadness in the passing of your beloved husband, Mr S R Nathan. The Labour Movement extends our deepest condolences to you and your family, and stands in solidarity with you during this time of mourning.

Mr Nathan was truly our brother-in-arms, workers' keeper, and people's leader, for he had always looked out for our interests. He once said, "The trade union movement is the place where the small man rises. The small man is important. Don't take him for granted." And he humbly added, "It's the trade union movement that gave me the courage to stand up and speak to big people without fear."

His indomitable and fearless fighting spirit in the 1960s, when he was with the National Trades Union Congress'

Labour Research Unit, helped win over workers' and unions' trust, including pro-communist unions, despite all political, economic, and social odds. He was all hands on when negotiating for workers and encouraged union leaders to stay rooted to the cause; be close to the ground; and change with the times with an eye for the future.

He showed union leaders what it meant to stand tall against irresponsible employers and be a responsible labour movement that prized co-operation over confrontation; and tripartism over self-interest. He was a people's leader who cared for us, and the Labour Movement was indeed honoured and proud to give him our strongest support when he stood to be the President of Singapore.

In May this year, when he visited NTUC, it was a homecoming for him as he was once again, among old friends and fellow union leaders. He was visibly happy and at times, fiery, when sharing his thoughts about our workers and Labour Movement. We will miss his inspiring stories and insightful lessons about being our brothers' and sisters' keeper, and how our Labour Movement needs to be at the forefront of economic and social changes so that benefits would go to all our people.

We will not forget his words, comradeship, and contributions. His leadership and legacy will remain with us for many generations of workers, union leaders, and Singaporeans to come.

Yours fraternally,

Mary Liew *Chan Chun Sing*
President *Secretary-General*

23 August 2016

Mdm Urmila Nandey

Dear Mrs Nathan,

We share your pain and sadness in the passing of your beloved husband, Mr S R Nathan. The Labour Movement extends our deepest condolences to you and your family and stands in solidarity with you during this time of mourning.

Mr Nathan was truly our brother-in-arms, workers' keeper and people's leader, for he had always looked out for our interests. He once said, "The trade union movement is the place where the small man rises. The small man is important. Don't take him for granted." And he humbly added, "It's the trade union movement that gave me the courage to stand up and speak to big people without fear."

His indomitable and fearless fighting spirit in the 1960s, when he was with the National Trades Union Congress' Labour Research Unit, helped win over workers' and unions' trust, including pro-communist unions, despite all political, economic and social odds. He was all hands on when negotiating for workers and encouraged union leaders to stay rooted to the cause; be close to the ground; and change with the times with an eye for the future.

He showed union leaders what it meant to stand tall against irresponsible employers and be a responsible labour movement that prized co-operation over confrontation; and tripartism over self-interest. He was a people's leader who cared for us and the Labour Movement was indeed honoured and proud to give him our strongest support when he stood to be the President of Singapore.

In May this year, when he visited NTUC, it was a homecoming for him as he was once again, among old friends and fellow union leaders. He was visibly happy and at times, fiery, when sharing his thoughts about our workers and Labour Movement. We will miss his inspiring stories and insightful lessons about being our brothers' and sisters' keeper and how our Labour Movement needs to be at the forefront of economic and social changes so that benefits would go to all our people.

We will not forget his words, comradeship and contributions. His leadership and legacy will remain with us for many generations of workers, union leaders and Singaporeans to come.

Yours fraternally,

Mary Liew
President

Chan Chun Sing
Secretary-General

Ms Mary Liew *is the President of the NTUC. Ms Liew was a former Nominated Member of Parliament.* **Mr Chan Chun Sing** *is the Secretary-General of the NTUC and is concurrently Minister in the Prime Minister's Office. This letter is reproduced with permission.*

MFA's Tribute to Mr S R Nathan

A MFA pioneer, Mr Nathan spent a large part of his distinguished career in the Foreign Service. In 1966, he joined the newly-minted Ministry as Assistant Secretary, and quickly rose to become Deputy Secretary (1967–1971). Mr Nathan returned to MFA as First Permanent Secretary from 1979–1982. Thereafter, he served as Singapore's High Commissioner to Malaysia (1988–1990) and Ambassador to the United States of America (1990–1996). In 1996, Mr Nathan took up the post of Ambassador-at-Large before being elected President of the Republic of Singapore in 1999.

As First Permanent Secretary, Mr Nathan instituted significant changes to improve professionalism in the fledging diplomatic service. In the 2008 inaugural S. Rajaratnam Lecture, he recalled: "We had no previous diplomatic experience or the institutional memory with which to engage in diplomacy. It was against those circumstances that our foreign policy had to be developed on the run, so to speak." Through Mr Nathan's leadership, MFA evolved into what he proudly called "a great enterprise made famous, despite our smallness". Mr Nathan's stint as High Commissioner to Malaysia coincided with a difficult time in bilateral ties. Given his long association with Malaysia and personal ties with its leaders, he deftly managed relations and kept things on an even keel. Mr Nathan also worked towards the signing of a new agreement in 1990, to supplement the 1962 Water Agreement. This new agreement led to the building of Linggiu Reservoir, which allows PUB to draw water from the Johor River, an important water source for Singaporeans. As Singapore's Ambassador to the United States, Mr Nathan adroitly steered bilateral relations during one of its controversial periods. Following the sentencing of American youth Michael Fay to caning in 1994, Singapore came under tremendous pressure from US politicians, the media, and NGOs who condemned the punishment. Mr Nathan was unfazed, showed tremendous dignity, and stoutly defended Singapore's position.

Mr Nathan once spoke about the qualities to be a successful diplomat. He singled out patience, calmness, modesty, empathy and good humour. He also said that foreign service officers must have "patriotism and sense of mission", "integrity and honesty", and the "ability to work under pressure". Mr Nathan embodied all these attributes and more. A diplomat *par excellence*, Mr Nathan was much loved, admired and respected for his warmth and compassion. In MFA, he was legendary for his ability to recall the names of everyone who had worked with him. He always had a kind word for his colleagues, no matter how senior or junior.

Mr Nathan has seen Singapore through many seminal moments. From social worker, unionist, bureaucrat to being elected to the highest office of the land, he is a defining part of the Singapore Story. We mourn the loss of one of Singapore's most distinguished sons.

This tribute was originally published on the website of Ministry of Foreign Affairs, Singapore. It is reproduced with permission.

Eulogy by Tommy Koh

MFA and Foreign Service

I have the honour to speak on behalf of the Ministry of Foreign Affairs and the Singapore Foreign Service. Mr Nathan had played a key role in the founding of both institutions. He joined the Ministry in December 1965 and helped our first Foreign Minister, Mr Rajaratnam, to set up the Ministry. He left in 1971 to assume another assignment. He returned in 1978 as its First Permanent Secretary. The Prime Minister had given him a mandate — transform the Ministry into a first class one in two years or it will be closed down and made into a department of the Prime Minister's Office. It seemed like a mission impossible. I had known Mr Nathan and worked closely with him since 1968. I regard him as my mentor and my comrade. In my eulogy, I will focus on the three enduring contributions which Mr Nathan had made.

From No Class to First Class

First, Mr Nathan succeeded in transforming the foreign Ministry, in two short years, from 'no class' to a first-class one. As we all know, Mr Lee Kuan Yew had very high standards. He made no allowances for the fact that our Ministry was new and we were all learning on the job. He expected the quality of our output to match the high standard of the centuries-old British Foreign Office. Undaunted by the challenge, Mr Nathan recruited bright young officers to join him. He demanded discipline, hard work, and competence. Most of all, he demanded loyalty and dedication to duty. His method of leadership was 'tough love'. However, behind that tough façade, there was a warm and kind heart. A few months ago, he hosted a lunch for about a dozen of the bright young officers, now grown old, who had helped him to fulfil his impossible mission. He wanted to thank them and to explain why he was such a demanding boss. It was a poignant occasion because we knew that it would be the last reunion with 'The Boss'. Because of the strong foundation he had laid, the Singapore Ministry of Foreign Affairs and the Singapore Foreign Service are considered among the best in the world.

Courage in the Face of Adversity

Second, he taught us to be courageous and to defend Singapore's interests without fear or hesitation. Mr Nathan was a courageous man as can be seen from his heroic role in the Laju case. He was our Ambassador in Washington at a difficult time. The Michael Fay case erupted during his watch. My American friends have told me that they admired the calm and rational way in which he defended Singapore's position in the face of vicious attacks. He held high the flag of Singapore. Because of his example and precept, although Singapore is a small country, it is a country which cannot be bullied by bigger countries, not even the major powers. One of the principles of Singapore's foreign policy is that it will stand up for its national interests against any foe, big or small.

Singapore's Super Ambassador

Third, Mr Nathan represented Singapore with great distinction as our High Commissioner to Malaysia and as our Ambassador to the United States. However, his most important diplomatic role was as the sixth President of Singapore. During his 12-year tenure, he visited more countries than all his predecessors put together. Through these state visits, he strengthened our links with other countries, expanded our political and economic space, and opened the door to new economic opportunities for our business and industry. He had a flair for dealing with foreign leaders and foreign countries. Perhaps because of his training in social work, he was able to establish a good rapport with his interlocutors and to put them at ease. He had the memory of an elephant and could remember people he had befriended in his previous assignments, no matter how long ago. He was able to convert his global network of friends into friends of Singapore.

Conclusion

I shall conclude. Mr Nathan will always be remembered as one of the founders of our Foreign Ministry and Foreign Service. Our success today is due to the strong foundation that he, Mr S. Rajaratnam, Mr Lee Kuan Yew, and other pioneers had laid. He taught us to be courageous and to be fearless in defending the national interests of Singapore. He was our super Ambassador to the world.

Ambassador Tommy Koh is currently Ambassador-at-Large, Ministry of Foreign Affairs. He is also the Special Adviser to the Institute of Policy Studies and a Professor of Law at the National University of Singapore. Ambassador Koh previously worked with Mr S R Nathan at the Ministry of Foreign Affairs. This eulogy is reproduced with permission.

A True Friend

Zainul A Rasheed

Many of us knew the late S R Nathan. Some knew him personally. His biography tells of how from a humble background, he climbed to the highest office in the land. He was a unionist, a public official, an ambassador, and finally the sixth President of Singapore. Since he was young, he had a determination to face the challenges of the world and determine for himself his life journey.

I believe that all of you are aware of his life successes. He was filled with the desire to sacrifice for the people around him and this beloved nation. His most poignant sacrifice was when he put his life on the line during the Laju Incident in January 1974.

I would like to share a few personal experiences I had with Mr Nathan through the years of our friendship.

I first came to know him in the early 1980s when I was 34 years old. He had just been appointed Executive Chairman of The Straits Times Press, and I was the Editor of *Berita Harian*.

I was still raw in the industry. At that time, I often met Mr Nathan. It was during this period that I received guidance from him, indirectly, on matters outside of journalism, especially in understanding human nature and various aspects of national and community development. It was knowledge that I did not learn in journalism school.

Mr Nathan's network of friends from his MINDEF and MFA days proved a boon when I was Associate Editor of *The Straits Times*. I was given the responsibility of setting up the paper's ASEAN Desk. The opportunities I had to accompany him on his visits to several ASEAN capitals to meet his former contacts, in and outside of government, had helped *The Straits Times* make inroads in the region.

When Mr Nathan became President, I was in MFA. I accompanied him on his visits to many countries in Africa, Asia, and the Middle East, including Kuwait. As someone who was directly involved in the Laju Incident which had ended in Kuwait, his visit helped to further strengthen the ties between both countries.

Mr Nathan was an extraordinary man. He walked with Kings, Sultans, Emirs, Presidents, and Prime Ministers, but in a special way, he retained the simple and ordinary in him. He was always his humble ordinary self with all of us. Mr Nathan was very much a man after our hearts.

Mr Nathan was someone who was very concerned about the affairs of the Malays. When I was Chairman of the Malay Heritage Foundation, Mr Nathan was able to raise $300,000 with just one lunch to finance the cost of publishing a book on Malay heritage.

Mr Nathan's commendable trait is that he respected his friends. Among his close friends was the late Haji Ridzwan Dzafir, who was a Director of Trade. Pak Wan, as he was fondly called, was also the President of the Islamic Religious Council (MUIS) and Chief Executive Officer of MENDAKI. Mr Nathan personally launched the biography of his old friend, in appreciation of his achievements and his contributions to Singapore.

Mr Nathan also took a personal interest in the Nagore Dargah monument project, which is now the Indian Muslim Heritage Centre. Truly, his concerns transcended race and religion.

Last May [in 2016], despite his ailing health, Mr Nathan attended the launch of the book *Majulah! 50 Years of the Malay/Muslim in Singapore.* He was very happy that the book had recorded the challenges and contributions of the Malay/Muslim community since Singapore's independence. He had always wanted Malays to see themselves as modern and fully-integrated Singaporeans, instead of just belonging to a minority.

The last time I had the opportunity to have a conversation with him was in July. For nearly an hour at SGH, he spoke to me about the affairs of Malays, a topic that was close to his heart.

For me, personally, I will not forget his love for food. This made our friendship closer. Just mention *briyani, nasi lemak*, and of course, durians, and a smile will light up his face.

I will long remember the days when we would have a chat while having tea and enjoying durian puffs at his residence in Ceylon Road. He was usually casually attired in his *sarong pelikat* at home.

Dear Mr Nathan, you will always be remembered. You have had more than a full life. You have achieved what others would not even have dared to dream of. You were a caring head of the family. You were a highly-dedicated top civil servant. You were a world-class diplomat. You were a People's President. And most importantly to me, you were a true friend.

Notwithstanding the long chats we have had about multiculturalism, religion, culture, heritage, leadership, and the contributions of the Malay/Muslim community to Singapore, I wished I had more time with you. When you were unconscious for the last few weeks, I had prayed hard to speak to you again. Many did. I could not resist it when Joseph Schooling won the Olympic Gold for our beloved Singapore. I knew you would be happy to hear that. Dressed in proud red and white shirt, I visited you in SGH, hoping hard that you would be better. When the nurse Siti Hidayah told me that she thought you responded when she sang *Majulah Singapura* to your ears, I whispered in your ears that you would be happy to know that Joseph Schooling had won the Olympic Gold for us, Singapore. It might have been wishful thinking, but at least I felt I had made you happy. We know how much you love Singapore. Mr Nathan, Rest in Peace.

Ambassador Zainul A Rasheed is Singapore's Non-Resident Ambassador to Kuwait and former Senior Minister of State for Foreign Affairs. Ambassador Zainul previously worked with Mr S R Nathan at The Straits Times Press, and subsequently, at Singapore Press Holdings when the latter was formed in 1984. This eulogy is reproduced with permission.

Lifelong Mentor and Friend

S Chandra Das

Mr S R Nathan has been a lifelong mentor to his associates and friends, myself included. I got to know Mr Nathan as a friend of the family in the late 1950s when I was a student at the Teachers' Training College. I came into official contact with him in the mid-1960s when I joined the Economic Development Board and he was with the Labour Research Unit. After he became a senior official in the fledgling Ministry of Foreign Affairs, I was with INTRACO engaged in trade negotiations with the Soviet Union and Eastern European states like Hungary from 1966; we were dealing with MFA on the diplomatic aspects of the trade agreements, and Mr Nathan became my mentor.

When I was appointed Singapore Trade Representative to Moscow, on secondment to MFA, in 1970, I benefitted from Mr Nathan's advice and guidance in carrying out my mission as the *de facto* Singapore diplomatic representative to the Soviet Union. I took instructions from him as Deputy Secretary of MFA while implementing INTRACO'S mandate in trade matters. He was meticulous and painstaking in briefing me on my diplomatic duties.

That included arranging and handling the first ever visit of Prime Minister Lee Kuan Yew in Autumn of 1970. Mr Nathan briefed me on what to do to ensure that the visit was a success, which covered 32 items of the Prime Minister's 'likes and dislikes'. These included a requirement that his bed must be hard and his preference for light German beer. As Mr Nathan had put it, we were all learning the ropes.

Beyond those mundane things, another tip was not to walk in front or behind Mr Lee but to be within eye range, to be able to catch his eye should he want something. An important point was to have a travel map with which to show the PM where he was at any given time. True enough, when we flew from Leningrad to Volgograd, the PM asked me where we were and I was able to whip out a map from my pocket and show him our flight path. My stock with him must have gone up!

During the visit, Mr Nathan showed by example what was expected of officials accompanying the PM. After the day's schedule of meetings with Soviet officials like PM Kosygin, Mr Nathan would type out his notes of the meetings and submit them to Mr Lee the next morning for clearance before sending a summary report back to DPM Goh Keng Swee in Singapore. That was the standard set by Mr Nathan which has been followed by MFA ever since. He was always willing to teach and share his experience in dealing with foreign officials and negotiations of trade agreements with East European states.

Mr Nathan's willingness to engage and share his experiences continued after I became a Member of

Parliament in the mid-1970s. He would meet Indian Community leaders to discuss the situation and challenges of the Indian community, particularly the poor and those left behind, and what could be done to uplift them. Out of these discussions came the setting up of SINDA, the Singapore Indian Development Association, of which Mr Nathan became a Trustee. He followed the progress and development of SINDA very closely. He was a great problem solver, good in analysis of the various courses of action to take and come out with solutions.

S R, as he was known to his associates, was very passionate in whatever project he undertook but ready to teach those who worked with him, even when he became President of Singapore. He made time to meet ordinary people and find ways to help those in need, regardless of their status or ethnicity. Indeed, he was accessible to all who sought his help or just wanted a picture taken with him. Mr Nathan had a lifelong devotion to education, having attained progress in work and life though his self-study and fortuitous admission to university for his Diploma in Social Studies. Towards the end of his presidency, it was his zeal for education for the disadvantaged that led him to set up an Education Upliftment Fund, to help the education of students and graduates of the Institutes of Technical Education (ITE) who were in need and had made the grade. The $9 million endowment fund is headed by accountant Bobby Chin, a member of the Council of Presidential Advisors.

Mr Nathan's unstinting support for scores of charities through the President's Challenge and other causes of the Community Chest are well documented. But not so well known are his acts of kindness for many destitute individuals and families whose plight or misfortune came to his notice. He would invariably source funds from a social organisation or altruistic individual to give them a helping hand. I was privileged to have assisted or worked with him in his various educational and community upliftment projects, such as SINDA, SOS, SIET, and Hindu Endowment Board.

When Mr Nathan was tasked to set up the Institute of Defence and Strategic Studies (IDSS), he asked me to chair the committee to raise funds for the S. Rajaratnam Endowment Fund, and worked with the committee to raise $26 million which was matched by the Government. The institute went on to become a distinguished graduate school, the S. Rajaratnam School of International Studies (RSIS), which President Nathan inaugurated in January 2007. Similarly, Mr Nathan promoted the building of the Indian Heritage Centre in Little India, funded by the Government, which paved the way for similar funding of the Malay, Chinese, and Eurasian Heritage Centres.

President Nathan was also Chancellor of National University of Singapore (NUS) and Nanyang Technological University (NTU), and presided over their growth and expansion. He also led the NUS in its annual inter-varsity game with the University of Malaya. Though he did not play golf, Mr Nathan gamely walked nine holes with his UM counterpart, Sultan Azlan Shah, then the King of Malaysia during several editions of the games. Thus did Mr Nathan perform as a Super Ambassador in further fostering friendly relations between the two neighbouring countries, which he had earlier done as

High Commissioner in the late 1980s. Of Mr Nathan it can be truly said — he walked with kings but lost not the common touch.

Mr Nathan asked me and another long-time associate, Gopinath Pillai, and our spouses to accompany him, Mrs Nathan and family on his private holiday trips to India. He was most gracious to us.

I also had the honour and privilege to organise his 80th, 85th, and 90th birthday parties on a grand scale. My only regret is not being able to help celebrate his 95th birthday.

Ambassador S Chandra Das is Singapore's Non-Resident High Commissioner to the Democratic Socialist Republic of Sri Lanka. Ambassador Das previously worked with Mr S R Nathan in various capacities.

Views from Abroad

The Unassuming Statesman
C Uday Bhaskar

In Memoriam: President S R Nathan, A Friend of Indonesia
Jusuf Wanandi

S R Nathan: A Friend in Deed
Kalimullah Hassan

S R Nathan's Academic World
Paul Evans

The Unassuming Statesman

C Uday Bhaskar

Singapore's former President S R Nathan, who passed away on August 22, was among the principal architects of the city-state along with the legendary Lee Kuan Yew. Among the less-known of his contributions (some of them bordering on the extraordinary) was building India–Singapore ties — and by extension, the Indo–ASEAN relationship that was at the core of Prime Minister Narasimha Rao's 'Look East' policy.

During the Cold War decades, India's relations with the Southeast Asian nations were, to put it mildly, frosty. Delhi saw the states in the region as parts of the US-led anti-communist block. "Coca-Cola republic" was one of the more sticky and, in hindsight, avoidable phrases of the Nehru years; the view from the other side about India was not too flattering either.

Indian diplomats who dealt with the region, and Singapore in particular, acknowledge that S R Nathan was the "real but silent mover behind the scenes" as far as the India–Singapore relationship was concerned. Subsequently, Singapore facilitated India's gradual, and at times grudging, acceptance by the Southeast Asian nations. Former secretary in the ministry of external affairs, Amarnath Ram, who had extensive dealings with the ASEAN, recalls S R Nathan as "an internationalist, an insightful thinker, respected intellectual, academic of high calibre and a humanist".

S R Nathan's role as one of the 'wise men' of the Council for Security Cooperation in the Asia Pacific (CSCAP) will long be remembered. He helped give direction and content to the CSCAP, particularly in its early years. He actively supported India in the CSCAP at a time when the country was considered an outsider in the Asia Pacific region.

My association with S R Nathan was brief but memorable. We first met in 1996 when he visited Delhi to study the IDSA, where I had just been appointed the deputy director. S R Nathan's formidable reputation preceded him, and I knew of him as Singapore's former ambassador to the US, and the former intelligence chief of his country. Here was a man who had faced severe personal setbacks during his formative years, saw the brutalities of World War II, and participated in the birth of Singapore. There were anecdotal references to the resolute manner with which he dealt with the communists and insurgents, and about his volunteering to be a hostage to resolve a Palestine terrorist-related crisis in 1974.

S R Nathan was visiting think tanks across the world, then, to observe the best practices — as he put it — for he was entrusted with the founding of Singapore's Institute of Defence and Strategic Studies (IDSS). S R Nathan, in his characteristically affable and unassuming manner, asked me to give him, what he described as, a "tutorial" about how the IDSA was run. He wanted to know the degree to which the research output of the institute actually contributed to, and shaped, government policy. Clearly, I was one among his many interlocutors and a relative greenhorn at that. But the earnest manner in which S R Nathan engaged with you made one feel very special.

One of the more tricky moments that he managed to defuse occurred in an India/ASEAN–ISIS conference in the mid-1990s in Delhi, where heads of all security think tanks of the ASEAN were invited. It was a major Track 1.5 effort, and the exchanges were candid. Given the history of the animus between India and the Southeast Asian nations, some discussions became very tense and heated. At one point, there was a near breakdown. S R Nathan stepped in, assuaged the bruised sensitivities and brought the conference back on track.

Appointed President of Singapore in 1999, S R Nathan was ever the gracious and generous host, and one will cherish calling on him in the Istana — the presidential palace. A role model for his citizens, S R Nathan was a man of many parts, and epitomised the diversity and dynamism of Singapore. It was a privilege to have met him — albeit very briefly.

Mr C Uday Bhaskar is a retired Commodore and one of India's leading experts on security and strategic affairs. This article was previously published in The Indian Express. It is reproduced with permission.

In Memoriam: President S R Nathan, A Friend of Indonesia

Jusuf Wanandi

I was late knowing about former Singapore President S R Nathan's passing because I was in Australia attending the Australian Council for Security Cooperation in the Asia Pacific's (CSCAP) annual general meeting.

President Nathan dealt with Indonesian affairs from the end of Indonesia's *Konfrontasi* against Malaysia in 1965, the year when Singapore separated from its union with Malaysia. He was then a member of the security team that prepared the opening of Singapore–Indonesia diplomatic relations. On the Indonesian side, it was Benny Moerdani and Abdul Rachman Ramly of Ali Moertopo's team who were his counterparts. That began his enduring interest in Indonesia, even when he was not in positions that directly related to the country, such as when he was Ambassador to the US and High Commissioner to Malaysia.

I fondly recall that when President Nathan was the head of The Straits Times Press, he and I occasionally took a morning walk along the beach near Mountbatten Road, and afterwards, had some coffee or a little breakfast at a hotel nearby.

During those walks, Indonesia–Singapore relations were always the main topic of our discussions. During his tenure as Director of the S. Rajaratnam School of International Studies (RSIS), he headed the Singapore CSCAP Committee, and we cooperated very closely in expanding CSCAP's programme to become a wider forum on security issues in East Asia and the Pacific, an extension of the biannual General Conference. He was convinced that the Track Two activities on regional security were a very important endeavour since the Track One (governments) cooperation only started after the end of the Cold War, and they needed more input and ideas from think tanks and other stakeholders like the media and political parties/parliaments. He was very attentive to the younger generations in Singapore and Indonesia, and was always keen to prepare them for their future leadership roles.

In that respect, President Nathan particularly found in me a soulmate, and he invited me to give a talk to his students at the Singapore Management University (SMU) on Indonesian experiences during the last years of the Sukarno era, the change of leadership, and the beginning of the Soeharto administration. He always believed that every young generation had to know more about its own and its neighbour's history. In addition, he graciously chaired the launching of my book *Shades of Grey* in 2012, also at SMU. I am eternally grateful to him for that honour and kindness.

As his health began to falter, our plan to continue the series of lectures was discontinued. However, in memory of President Nathan, I will make myself available to keep the plan alive, especially as an effort to strengthen Indonesia–Singapore relations. Our bilateral cooperation inside and outside of ASEAN is important and will contribute to an East Asia that is stable, peaceful, and developing well. Indonesia and Singapore complement each other in many aspects, which really contribute to that purpose. My experiences in building regional institutions within the context of the ASEAN Institute of Strategic and International Studies (ISIS) and other regional institutions convinced me of the critical importance of Indonesia–Singapore cooperation. So, talking about strengthening ASEAN and how to keep ASEAN's centrality in the wider Asia Pacific region, I think Indonesia–Singapore cooperation is a prerequisite. And I believe that somewhere there, President Nathan would agree with me.

From President Nathan, I found out that many Singaporean leaders were sympathetic to Indonesia, obviously because of Indonesia's size and influence as a neighbour, but also as Singapore can learn from Indonesia's diversity, self-confidence despite the challenges it has to face, and its foreign policy character, which Singapore can emulate as a young and small country proud of its independence among other big countries. Together, Indonesia and Singapore can do more to create better neighbourliness despite existing negative stereotypes about each other. That can be remedied by better understanding between the two countries. May President Nathan rest in peace, and may Mrs Urmila Nandi and the whole family be strengthened in their loss.

Mr Jusuf Wanandi is a Senior Fellow and co-founder of the Centre for Strategic and International Studies (CSIS), and Vice Chairman of the Board of Trustees CSIS Foundation, Jakarta. This article was previously published in The Jakarta Post Daily and is reproduced with permission.

S R Nathan: A Friend in Deed

Kalimullah Hassan

It was a humid morning on September 16, 1988 that I first met the late Mr S R Nathan in Kota Kinabalu, Sabah. We were all gathered at the Padang for the flag-raising ceremony to celebrate Malaysia Day — the date Sabah, Sarawak and Singapore with Malaya formed the federation of Malaysia in 1963.

Then Deputy Prime Minister Ghafar Baba was the guest-of-honour, unveiling the new state flag, and I was his Press Secretary. Nathan, who had a few months earlier been appointed as Singapore's High Commissioner to Malaysia, was among the many dignitaries and diplomats present.

Prior to my appointment as Ghafar's secretary, I had been a Pressman with local newspapers such as *The Star* and the *New Straits Times* and later, as a correspondent with the Reuters bureau in Kuala Lumpur where I interacted a lot with diplomats. Among them, one of my closest friends was Verghese Mathews, a First Secretary with the Singapore High Commission.

The foreign correspondents used to have weekly drinks at a French restaurant called La Terrasse, directly opposite the Singapore High Commission in Kuala Lumpur.

When news of Nathan's appointment first reached us in Kuala Lumpur, stories swirled about his previous job as head of Singapore intelligence and how he was "sent" to The Straits Times Press as Executive Chairman to ensure editorial policy was aligned to the PAP's political interests. (These issues are addressed frankly by Nathan in his biography, *An Unexpected Journey*, but at that time, such nuggets of information, when there was no internet and blogs, were juicy topics of conversation, and much embellished over endless mugs of beer).

Mathews, who had served under Nathan in the Foreign Ministry, always spoke highly of him. It was against this backdrop that I saw the man, S R Nathan, looking dapper in the sweltering heat of Kota Kinabalu.

Relations between Malaysia and Singapore in those days were always testy and although I was a junior cog in the Government machinery, I was, still, an aide to the second most powerful man in the Malaysian Government. However, as far as I recall, I was not the least bit wary when I spoke to him during the ceremony because much as I knew Nathan was 100 per cent a Singapore loyalist, I was equally confident of my loyalties as a Malaysian. There was a healthy respect for each other, which marked our relationship over the years.

My first impression of Nathan has stayed with me all the while — almost three decades later. As Singapore's top diplomat in Malaysia, formerly a confidant of Singapore's Prime Minister Lee Kuan Yew and head of his country's intelligence service, and Executive Chairman of The Straits Times Press, Nathan displayed none of the haughtiness and arrogance that I have seen in lesser officials on both sides of the Causeway, then and now.

It struck me that despite his achievements, Nathan displayed a humility that was refreshing. He was more than twice my age then, and yet, he spoke to me kindly, and as an equal. That endeared me to him, and during his stint as High Commissioner, we would continue to meet many more times on a social and professional basis, mainly with a small tight-knit group of foreign correspondents and senior local journalists.

Not long after that meeting, I had to leave my job as Press Secretary. The late Ghafar Baba, a wonderful man, though less highly regarded because of the comparisons made with his boss, the mercurial but brilliant Dr Mahathir Mohamad, one day called me in to his office and told me he wanted me to return to the media, saying that there were reasons he could not confirm me in my job. He declined to go into these reasons but said: "You have been the best Press Secretary I ever had in all my years in public service. If there is anything I can do to help you, just let me know."

Ghafar was a man of few words, and although I maintained my relations with him until his death, he never told me why I had to leave. I heard from his then political secretary Kamaruddin Jaafar that some UMNO

Youth leaders had asked Ghafar why he had appointed a non-Malay (I am a Malaysian, born and bred, but ethnically, I am a Pathan, or an Indian Muslim) as his Press Secretary. Ghafar's reply, according to Kamaruddin who was present when these concerns were raised, was that I was capable and I was loyal. The other persistent rumour was that the Special Branch had not given me security clearance because I was too close to foreign diplomats, in particular, Singaporeans.

Ghafar told me to stay on until I found a new job, but weeks later, I decided to leave. It was a tumultuous time in Malaysian politics. Mahathir had just survived a leadership challenge and UMNO leaders were paranoid. I worried that if there was a leak, as I had access in my job to information at the highest levels of Government, suspicion would fall on me.

After resigning, my friends like Ismail Kassim, who was *The Straits Times* correspondent in Kuala Lumpur, and others in the foreign Press, helped me get freelance jobs for *The Straits Times* and *Time* magazine. It was not a good time in my life but thankfully, my wife, a lawyer, had a steady job and we survived.

The Straits Times, aware of the rumours, was not inclined to give me a permanent job because they feared repercussions, given the edgy Malaysia–Singapore relations and politics of that time. Even as a stringer, or freelancer, the Human Resource manager at that time insisted I obtain a letter from Ghafar recommending me for the job. I went to see Ghafar and he told me: "You prepare the letter and I will sign it."

It was surreal. I went back to my old office and drafted a letter on the Deputy Prime Minister's letterhead and went back to his room. Ghafar, God bless his soul, signed the letter and told me to see him again if I had problems. On the strength of that letter, *The Straits Times* offered me a job as a stringer.

As a stringer, I was paid for the articles I wrote and which were used by the newspaper. However, there was no certainty and it was difficult to plan ahead. I could not even get a loan to buy a house because I did not have a fixed income stream.

Some months later, Nathan asked me to a meal to find out how I was coping. He then asked why *The Straits Times* had not offered me a full-time job despite my experience, and I explained. Nathan was upset and said he would have a word with *The Straits Times*. Not long after that, I was offered a full-time job as Kuala Lumpur correspondent. I will always be grateful to Nathan for that.

Subsequently, Nathan, too, had to leave his post as High Commissioner. In his book, he says that the Malaysian intelligence services and Dr Mahathir suspected him of being involved in espionage.

Nathan was re-assigned as Singapore's Ambassador to Washington. One day, Verghese Mathews told me that Nathan had had a heart bypass operation, and I flew to Singapore to visit him. He was touched and very appreciative. Eventually, he retired as Ambassador and returned to Singapore to contest, and became President of Singapore.

As the wheel turns, many years later, my friend Abdullah Ahmad Badawi, for whom Nathan has only nice things to say, became Deputy Prime Minister and Home Minister of Malaysia. I had also moved on, quitting my job at *The Straits Times* in 1995, and went into business. I had virtually no contact with Nathan during this period, but we would keep abreast of each other's progress and well-being through friends like Mathews and others.

In 2002, Abdullah asked me to become Chairman of the national news agency, *Bernama*. I was hesitant and told Abdullah that the ghosts of the past — the inference of my alleged links to Singapore — might not be good for him politically. I still remember what Abdullah said to me.

"Kali — I am Home Minister. Don't you think I have already checked out my friends?"

It was when Abdullah became Prime Minister in 2003 that relations with Singapore began to improve and have continued to be enhanced under his successor Najib Tun Razak.

Shortly after he became Prime Minister, Abdullah asked me to take on the job as Editor-in-Chief of then the largest newspaper group in the country, the *New Straits Times*. I put my corporate career on hold and started my job in 2004 where I wrote a weekly column in the *New Sunday Times*.

(One day, I wrote a column about my friend Jack Choo, who had served under Nathan as Counsellor in the High Commission in Kuala Lumpur. Jack had just passed away from cancer. He, too, was a victim of the Singapore–Malaysia Cold War years. While serving in Malaysia, he had fallen in love with a senior officer of the Malaysian Education Ministry, Fatimah, and when they decided to get married, both had their security clearances suspended. Both eventually left the civil service, and started a small beach resort in Kuantan, Pahang, where Jack eventually passed away. Nathan read my column and sent me a handwritten note, reminiscing fondly about Jack.)

Months later, Nathan made an official visit to Malaysia and requested to see me at a reception hosted by the High Commission at the Mandarin Oriental. Of course, I attended and though we did not spend much time, we were both happy to see how each other had gone on to better things in service of our countries.

In 2007, I had to undergo a major spinal surgery in Mount Elizabeth Hospital in Singapore. While recuperating, I got a call from the Istana. Nathan wanted to visit, and he fixed a time to see me the next day. I was pleased but did not think much of it until the CEO of the hospital, Tan See Leng, came to my room, hassled and in a flux, asking me to keep him informed because "he is the President of Singapore, you know…".

As it is, Nathan could not visit because he had developed a cold, and said he did not want to pass it to me. He called me to wish me well and said that I should visit him for lunch when I was in Singapore next. Again, in December 2014, when I had another major spinal surgery in Singapore, Nathan again called to wish me a speedy recovery. But, by this time, he was already not well and apologised for not being able to visit. I was in the hospital for several weeks due to complications arising out of the surgery, but it was encouraging words from friends like Nathan that kept me going.

I was semi-paralysed after the surgery and have been undergoing intense physiotherapy to recover use of my limbs in the last two years. I am still not steady on my feet and have had to make major lifestyle changes, but have been walking without a cane since March 2016.

During this time, we kept in touch through friends, and when Nathan became ill, I wanted to fly to Singapore to visit him, but was told that visitations were restricted. Unfortunately, he passed away and it is my regret that I could not see him one last time.

I had often wondered why Nathan was so kind to me. It was not until I read his book that I had an inkling of the man, beyond his much talked-about role as head of intelligence and confidant of Lee Kuan Yew.

He would always revel us with stories of his growing up years in Muar, and of the barber, Alagoo. Nathan once told us about the time he returned to Muar when he was a senior Government official and how, in his honour, Alagoo served him rum. Nathan tasted it and asked: "What is this?" Much to his amusement, perhaps horror, he found out it was not Jamaican rum but rather the cheap alcohol Indian barbers use as a substitute for cologne, that he was being served.

In his autobiography, Nathan talks about the people who had helped him when he had nothing but the shirt on his back — people like Alagoo, the Japanese army officer Lieutenant Kokubu, his Indian Muslim friend Kader, or Nana, and his Malay friend Noordin. They protected him and gave him advice which would mould his character to become one of Singapore's most powerful and trusted public servants.

He never forgot these friends and visited them when he was in high office, maintaining relationships. Perhaps, I think, he saw in me that evening in 1988, a kindred soul who needed a leg up in life and he provided me that support, cutting through the Cold-War mindset and bureaucracy, to get me the full-time job as correspondent in *The Straits Times*.

The lessons I learnt from Nathan have stood me in good stead over the years, and in some ways, have made me relatively successful in life. In many ways, I try to do the same, by remembering my friends, and by helping those that I can through a foundation my partner Lim Kian Onn and I set up and manage.

A good example is Abdullah Ahmad Badawi. When he was sacked from the Cabinet in 1987, and his friends and at times even family, shunned him, I remained a friend, helping draft his speeches and arranging for visiting correspondents to interview him and keep him in the public eye. Many years later, when he became Deputy Prime Minister and Prime Minister, Abdullah recognised that friendship and vindicated me by appointing me to positions of public office, despite the insidious whispers about my loyalty to my country.

I am proud to count Abdullah as my friend. And I am proud to count Nathan as my friend. In my book, they are both among the "few good men".

Dato Seri Kalimullah Hassan *was the former Deputy Chairman and Editor-in-Chief of the New Straits Times Press, and the former Press Secretary of the Deputy Prime Minister of Malaysia.*

S R Nathan's Academic World

Paul Evans

I first met S R Nathan in late 1996 at a meeting hosted by the Council for Security Cooperation in Asia Pacific (CSCAP). It was at the time he was establishing the Institute of Defence and Security Studies (IDSS) and looking for ways to connect it to the regional dialogue and research networks then in a creative period of development.

While few of us non-Singaporean academics in the Track Two world knew him personally, all of us knew of him by reputation for his roles in the Ministries of Foreign Affairs and Defence, his ambassadorial postings, his involvement in security and intelligence affairs, and even as the hero in the 1974 Shell refinery ferry hijacking.

It was a surprise when he offered a precise comment on something I had said in the workshop and suggested a private meeting to discuss what he had in mind for IDSS. In that meeting, he asked a series of probing questions about how the Institute could avoid too heavy a reliance on the British institutions that were already playing a leading role in shaping his Institute, and the American think tanks and universities that so heavily influenced global standards. He had clear and direct views about what he saw as the Canadian role in global affairs, its recent initiatives in the region based on a constructive interaction between academics (who did not rotate in and out of government) and officials, and the hybrid character of Canadian universities that incorporated elements of both the American and British systems.

How did we do Track Two? How and why did our government support it? Why did some of our top international relations scholars want to participate in it? Did it contribute to their careers or impair them? The questions were crisp, direct, and looked to answers that were likewise devoid of palaver.

I do not remember him asking an idle question without a strategic purpose and a presumed, though flexible, answer in his own mind. More than one colleague said that speaking with him was like speaking with Henry Kissinger, an exercise in constant and multi-dimensional calculation.

In the formative years of IDSS and during his time as President, we met on several occasions for private conversations. After departing the Presidency and connecting with various academic institutions, we met more frequently and in more relaxed surroundings. We talked broadly about regional and local political developments, leaders and personalities, the ingredients and implications of China's rise, and Singapore's past and future. I discovered he liked direct opinions, was curious, and did not shy away from challenging ideas he thought wrong or misleading.

In 2013, he encouraged me to develop a workshop at Singapore Management University (SMU) on Singapore's foreign policy with the intention of creating a conversation between students and experienced officials and leaders, himself among them. When I told him I knew very little about the subject, he replied that this was my chance to learn more and that the outsider's view of an empathetic Canadian could open up a subject that was not being addressed at any other institution in the country.

In his three annual sessions with the students, he struck a tone that was at once avuncular and blunt. He rejected the idea that Singaporean students were uninterested in foreign affairs, but felt they knew too little about the subject, including the enduring principles and lived reality of the pioneer generation. For the most part, the students were polite and listened with care and a touch of reverence. However, he was correct in his view that there was a generational gap that was very hard for him to bridge.

S R Nathan did not consider himself an academic or an intellectual, though he had a penetrating intelligence and a shrewd ability to create an academic institution at the interface of teaching, research and strategic impact. In *The Unexpected Journey*, he repeats admiringly Tony Tan's analogy for why strategy needed a strong intellectual base: "Strategy can be compared to the mind — it is the intellectual basis for what you do; tactical competence is the legs, getting you where you want to be; and technical competence, like the human arm, allows you to execute policy once you get there" (Nathan 2011, 604).

At both IDSS and SMU, he emphasised the need for combining research and teaching, encouraging faculty to keep sharp by being challenged by students. He did not care for or debate theory, books or journals, but instead experiences, political choices, and personal character. Shrewd, rationalistic, and direct, he based his estimation of academics not on what they wrote, but on their accumulated reputation and the value of what he heard them say. He deeply enjoyed his interaction with academics at their best and had a high appreciation of what they could contribute while not unaware of their occasional frailties.

In our last conversations a few months before his death in August, he expressed worries about the United States and what he saw as its gathering retreat into isolationism and populism. He was also worried about China's overbearing nature. He felt religious extremism, Wahhabism in particular, was the biggest external threat in Singapore's neighbourhood. He also spoke about how Singapore needed to recapture its sense of national purpose, and how quickly the world would lose interest in it if its economy faltered.

A realist by experience rather than formal education, a person who prized and cultivated human relations, someone who did not believe in progress but who was not entirely gloomy about the future, he created a fertile garden in which the academic enterprise and the inquiring mind could take root.

Professor Paul Evans *is a professor at the University of British Columbia, and is concurrently the Lee Kong Chian Visiting Professor at the Singapore Management University.*

Condolence Messages
from Southeast Asia

Negara Brunei Darussalam

Kingdom of Cambodia

Republic of Indonesia

Lao People's Democratic Republic

Malaysia

Republic of the Union of Myanmar

Republic of the Philippines

Kingdom of Thailand

Socialist Republic of Vietnam

Negara Brunei Darussalam

On behalf of the Government and people of His Majesty the Sultan and Yang Di-Pertuan of Brunei Darussalam, please accept our deepest condolences to the Government and people of the Republic of Singapore and to the family of His Excellency S R Nathan.

Pehin Dato Lim Jock Seng
Minister at the Prime Minister's Office
and Minister of Foreign Affairs and Trade II

From **HE Pehin Dato Lim Jock Seng**, Minister at the Prime Minister's Office and Second Minister of Foreign Affairs and Trade, Negara Brunei Darussalam.

Kingdom of Cambodia

Having served as Senior Minister, Deputy Prime Minister and Foreign Minister for more than 20 years, I have had the honour to meet and pay courtesy call, on several occasions, on H.E. Mr. S.R. NATHAN, Former President of the Republic of Singapore who was a very wise Statesman.

On this very sad occasion, may I express my profound condolences and very deepest sympathy to the bereaved family and the people of Singapore.

HOR Namhong
Deputy Prime Minister

---

*From **HE Hor Namhong**, Deputy Prime Minister, Kingdom of Cambodia.*

Republic of Indonesia

"My deepest respect to President S.R. Nathan — a great son of Singapore & a great friend of Indonesia. We will sorely miss him, and we are forever indebted to you Mr. Nathan, for your tireless endeavor to the cause of peace and friendship among nations"

Jakarta, 25 August 2016

DR. S. B. YUDHOYONO
FORMER PRESIDENT OF INDONESIA

---

*From **Dr H Susilo Bambang Yudhoyono**, Sixth President of the Republic of Indonesia.*

Lao People's Democratic Republic

On behalf of the Government and the people of the Lao's people Democratic Republic, I would like to express my deepest condolences upon the passing away of H.E.S.R Nathan, Former President of the Republic of Singapore.

The demise of H.E.S.R Nathan caused the grieved loss of an outstanding leader who significantly contributed to the development of Singapore over the past decades.

We would like to share this moment of sadness and sympathy with the Government and the People of Singapore as well as with the bereaved family.

Vientiane, 24 August 2016

Khamphao ERNTHAVANH

From **HE Mdm Khamphao Ernthavanh**, *Vice Minister of Foreign Affairs, Lao People's Democratic Republic.*

Malaysia

On behalf of the Government and the people of Malaysia, let me express our heartfelt condolences to the family of the late Mr SR Nathan, former President of Singapore.

When he was High Commissioner in KL and later as President, the late President Nathan was a great advocate of closer ties between Malaysia and Singapore. For this we appreciate his many contributions.

May his soul rest in peace.

26/8/16

From **YAB Dato Sri Mohd Najib bin Tun Abdul Razak**, *Prime Minister, and Minister of Finance, Malaysia.*

Republic of the Union of Myanmar

25 August 2016

The Ministry of Foreign Affairs of Myanmar expresses its deep condolences to the Embassy of Singapore in Yangon and through the Embassy to the bereaved family of the late President of Singapore H.E S R Nathan. H.E. S.R Nathan was a great leader and an ideal diplomat of Singapore. He will be remembered as a great statesman who dedicated himself for the cause of the country and promoted friendship between Singapore and the countries in the world.

AUNG LYNN
Permanent Secretary
MOFA NayPyiTaw

---

*From **HE U Aung Lynn**, Ambassador Extraordinary, and Plenipotentiary of the Republic of the Union of Myanmar to the United States of America (then-Permanent Secretary of the Ministry of Foreign Affairs).*

Republic of the Philippines

On behalf of the Filipino people, I extend my profound and heartfelt condolences to the people of Singapore for the passing of President S. R. Nathan. An exemplary public servant, President Nathan was the embodiment of duty and honor in furthering Singapore's growth and prosperity. His dedication and service to his country are engraved in the hearts of the people, and his legacy will live on in the annals of Singapore's proud history.

Our thoughts and prayers go out to his family during this time of mourning.

Ma. Hellen B. De La Vega
Assistant Secretary, ASEAN
DFA-Philippines
26 August 2016

---

*From HE **Ambassador Ma Hellen B De La Vega**, Assistant Secretary, Office of ASEAN Affairs, Department of Foreign Affairs, Republic of the Philippines.*

Kingdom of Thailand

His Royal Highness Crown Prince Maha Vajiralongkorn has commanded me to convey his sympathy and condolences on the demise of Mr. SR Nathan

ACM Kasem Yoosuk RTAF
Chief, private secretary office of the
H.R.H. the Crown Prince of Thailand.

---

*From **ACM Kasem Yoosuk**, Chief Private Secretary, on behalf of **His Majesty King Maha Vajiralongkorn Bodindradebayavarangkun** (then-His Royal Highness Crown Prince), Kingdom of Thailand.*

This is the message from the Prime Minister

"Excellency,

You had been a great friend of Thailand, bilaterally and as a family member of ASEAN. We salute your great achievements all through your many years in the highest office of Singapore. Our condolences to the bereaved family members and the people of Republic of Singapore for this great loss!

Please rest easy in Peace!

From **HE Don Pramudwinai**, *Minister of Foreign Affairs, on behalf of HE Prime Minister* **General Prayut Chan-o-cha**, *Kingdom of Thailand.*

Socialist Republic of Vietnam

Hà nội, ngày 24/8/2016

Vô cùng thương tiếc Ngài S R Nathan, nguyên Tổng thống nước Cộng hòa Singapore. Việt Nam chia sẻ mất mát to lớn này với Nhà nước, Chính phủ, nhân dân Singapore và Gia quyến Ngài S.R. Nathan.

Chủ nhiệm
Văn phòng Chủ tịch nước
Nước CHXHCN Việt Nam

Đào Việt Trung

From **HE Dao Viet Trung**, *Chairman of President's Office, Socialist Republic of Vietnam.*

Pictures

Mr Nathan, the Family Man

Mr Nathan, the Distinguished Civil Servant

Mr Nathan, the People's President

Mr Nathan, a Mentor for All Seasons

Mr Nathan, the Family Man

President S R Nathan and Mrs Nathan. Picture courtesy of the Nathan family.

Mr S R Nathan, Director of the Security and Intelligence Division, being greeted by his wife and children upon arrival at the Paya Lebar Airport, following the end of the Laju hijack crisis (February 9, 1974). Source: *The Straits Times* © Singapore Press Holdings Limited. Reprinted with permission.

President S R Nathan and his grandchildren, Monisha, Kiron, and Kheshin (standing from left to right). Picture courtesy of the Nathan family.

Mr S R Nathan, Mrs Nathan, Monisha, Mr Nathan's granddaughter, and Juthika, Mr Nathan's daughter. Picture courtesy of the Nathan family.

Mr S R Nathan and Mrs Nathan with their grandchildren, Kiron, Monisha and Kheshin (from left to right) during Mr Nathan's 90th birthday celebrations in July 2014. Picture courtesy of the Nathan family.

Mr Nathan, the Distinguished Civil Servant

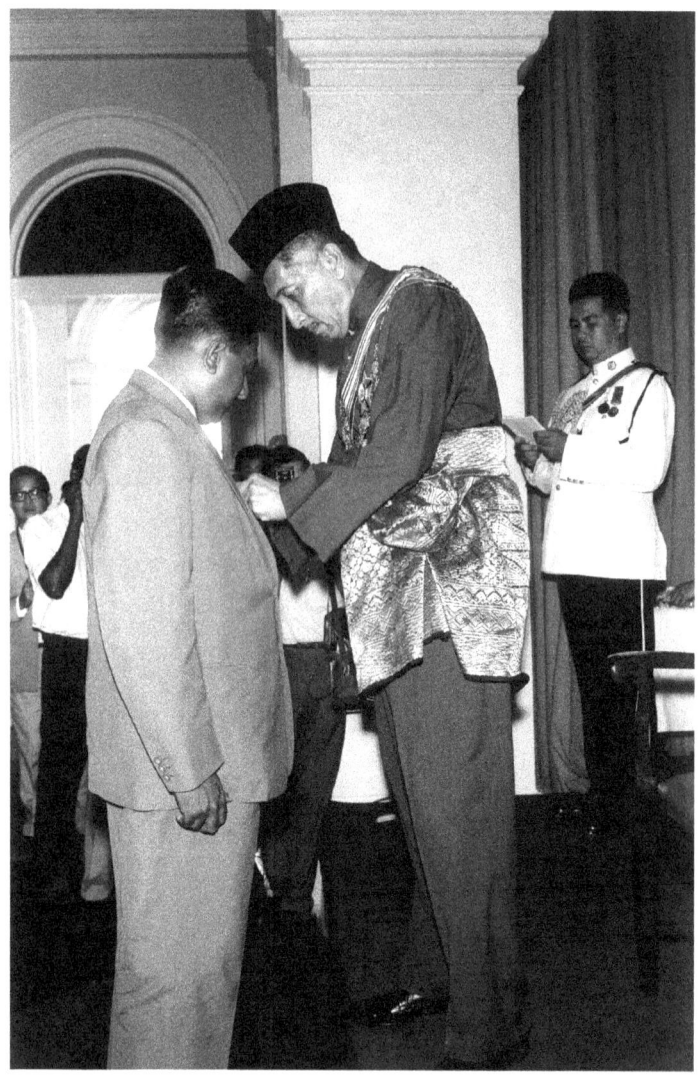

Mr S R Nathan, Director of the Labour Research Unit, receiving the Public Service Star (Bintang Bakti Masyarakat), from Yang di-Pertuan Negara of Singapore Yusof Ishak at the investiture ceremony in 1964, held at the Istana Negara. Source: Ministry of Information, Communications and the Arts Collection, courtesy of the National Archives of Singapore. Reprinted with permission.

Mr S R Nathan, Director of the Security and Intelligence Division, welcoming President Suharto of Indonesia upon his arrival at the Paya Lebar Airport for a three-day state visit to Singapore in 1974. Behind President Suharto is President Dr Benjamin Henry Sheares. Source: Ministry of Information, Communications and the Arts Collection, courtesy of the National Archives of Singapore. Reprinted with permission.

The 13 Singapore Government Officials at a Press Conference held at the Paya Lebar Airport upon their arrival from Kuwait. They had left Singapore for Kuwait on a special Japan Air Lines flight as guarantors of safe passage for the hijackers during the Laju incident in 1974. The team was headed by Mr S R Nathan, Director of the Security and Intelligence Division. Source: *The Straits Times* © Singapore Press Holdings Limited. Reprinted with permission.

Mr S R Nathan, Director of Security and Intelligence Division, receiving the Meritorious Service Medal (*Pingat Jasa Gemilang*), the highest honour given in 1974, from President Dr Benjamin Henry Sheares at the Investiture of 1974 National Day awards, held at the Singapore Conference Hall. Source: Ministry of Information, Communications and the Arts Collection, courtesy of the National Archives of Singapore. Reprinted with permission.

Mr S R Nathan, First Permanent Secretary, Ministry of Foreign Affairs, bidding farewell to Sultan Hassanal Bolkiah of Negara Brunei Darussalam, at the Paya Lebar Airport, in 1980, along with other government officials. Source: Ministry of Information, Communications and the Arts Collection, courtesy of the National Archives of Singapore. Reprinted with permission.

Mr S R Nathan, Executive Chairman of The Straits Times Press, with Second Deputy Prime Minister (Foreign Affairs) Mr S. Rajaratnam attending a conference on 'Investment Opportunities in Turbulent Times', held at the Shangri-La Hotel in 1983. Source: Ministry of Information, Communications and the Arts Collection, courtesy of the National Archives of Singapore. Reprinted with permission.

Mr S R Nathan, Executive Chairman of The Straits Times Press, giving a speech at the Pre-University Seminar, 'Birth of a Nation: Singapore in the 1950s', held at Nanyang Technological Institute in 1984. Source: Ministry of Information, Communications and the Arts Collection, courtesy of the National Archives of Singapore. Reprinted with permission.

Mr S R Nathan, Executive Chairman of The Straits Times Press, with Minister for Finance Dr Richard Hu Tsu Tau arrives at the Shangri-La Hotel to attend 1987 Businessman of the Year Award presentation and dinner. Source: Ministry of Information, Communications and the Arts Collection, courtesy of the National Archives of Singapore. Reprinted with permission.

When Mr S R Nathan was High Commissioner in Malaysia (1988 to 1990), he kept in touch with Singapore pensioners in Malacca. Picture from Ambassador Ong Keng Yong's personal collection.

High Commissioner S R Nathan with Foreign Minister of Singapore, Mr Wong Kan Seng at the Singapore High Commission in Kuala Lumpur during an official visit to Malaysia in 1989. Picture from Ambassador Ong Keng Yong's personal collection.

High Commissioner S R Nathan and Foreign Minister of Malaysia Abu Hassan Omar (on the right of Mr Nathan) arriving for an official dinner organised by the Singapore High Commissioner in Kuala Lumpur in 1989. Picture from Ambassador Ong Keng Yong's personal collection.

President Wee Kim Wee presenting Ambassador-Designate to the United States of America, Mr S R Nathan, his Letter of Credence at the Istana in September 1990. Source: Istana Collection, courtesy of the National Archives of Singapore. Reprinted with permission.

Ambassador S R Nathan and Mrs Nathan with Foreign Minister Wong Kan Seng (fifth from left) and Mrs Wong (fourth from left), at the official opening of the new premises of the Singapore Embassy in Washington DC in 1993. Picture from Ambassador Ong Keng Yong's personal collection.

Ambassador S R Nathan and Mrs Nathan with ladies from the Singapore Embassy in Washington, DC visiting Blacksburg in Virginia in 1993. The ladies participated in a culinary event there to show off Singaporean food. Picture from Ambassador Ong Keng Yong's personal collection.

Celebrating Mr S R Nathan's birthday with Mrs Nathan in Washington, DC, July 1992. Picture from Ambassador Ong Keng Yong's personal collection.

Mr S R Nathan, Director of the Institute of Defence and Strategic Studies (IDSS), receiving Guest-of-Honour, Dr Tony Tan Keng Yam, Deputy Prime Minister and Minister for Defence, Singapore at the inaugural Asia Pacific Programme for Senior Military Officers (APPSMO) in 1999.

Mr Nathan, the People's President

Mr S R Nathan, presidential candidate, greeting supporters at People's Association in Kallang on Nomination Day in 1999. Source: Ministry of Information, Communications and the Arts Collection, courtesy of the National Archives of Singapore. Reprinted with permission.

President Ong Teng Cheong hosting a lunch for former President Wee Kim Wee and President-Elect S R Nathan at the President's Lounge, Istana in 1999. Source: Ministry of Information, Communications and the Arts Collection, courtesy of the National Archives of Singapore. Reprinted with permission.

President S R Nathan mingling with students at the opening of the Second Session of the Ninth Parliament in 1999. Source: Ministry of Information, Communications and the Arts Collection, courtesy of the National Archives of Singapore. Reprinted with permission.

President S R Nathan meets a group of primary school children at the President's Lounge, Istana, in 1999. Source: Ministry of Information, Communications and the Arts Collection, courtesy of the National Archives of Singapore. Reprinted with permission.

President S R Nathan attends a Mid-Autumn Festival celebration in 1999, organised by the Singapore Chinese Chamber of Commerce and Industry. Source: Ministry of Information, Communications and the Arts Collection, courtesy of the National Archives of Singapore. Reprinted with permission.

President S R Nathan launches a fund-raiser, organised by Tabung Amal Aidilfitri in 1999. Source: Ministry of Information, Communications and the Arts Collection, courtesy of the National Archives of Singapore. Reprinted with permission.

President S R Nathan attends a tea reception at the Eurasian Association Community House in 1999. Source: Ministry of Information, Communications and the Arts Collection, courtesy of the National Archives of Singapore. Reprinted with permission.

President S R Nathan meets visitors at the Istana during the Open House on Chinese New Year, 2000. Source: Ministry of Information, Communications and the Arts Collection, courtesy of the National Archives of Singapore. Reprinted with permission.

United Nations Secretary-General Kofi A Annan calling on President S R Nathan in 2000. Source: Ministry of Information, Communications and the Arts Collection, courtesy of the National Archives of Singapore. Reprinted with permission.

President S R Nathan at the Singapore Scout Association Rally in 2000, held at Catholic High School. Source: Ministry of Information, Communications and the Arts Collection, courtesy of the National Archives of Singapore. Reprinted with permission.

President S R Nathan as Guest-of-Honour at a dinner hosted by the Indian Community at the Shangri-La Hotel Ballroom in 2000. Source: Ministry of Information, Communications and the Arts Collection, courtesy of the National Archives of Singapore. Reprinted with permission.

President S R Nathan attends the President's Challenge Charity Walk at the Padang in 2000. Source: Ministry of Information, Communications and the Arts Collection, courtesy of the National Archives of Singapore. Reprinted with permission.

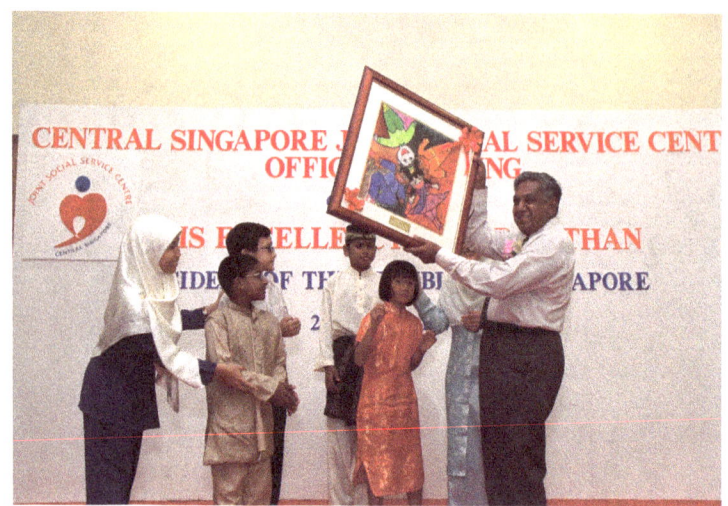

President S R Nathan officiates at the Opening Ceremony of the Central Singapore Joint Social Service Centre (JSSC) in 2000. Source: Ministry of Information, Communications and the Arts Collection, courtesy of the National Archives of Singapore. Reprinted with permission.

President S R Nathan visits the Scient Cyber Teens Demonstration at Suntec City in December 2000. Source: Ministry of Information, Communications and the Arts Collection, courtesy of the National Archives of Singapore. Reprinted with permission.

President S R Nathan visits Tengah Airbase in 2002. Source: Ministry of Information, Communications and the Arts Collection, courtesy of the National Archives of Singapore. Reprinted with permission.

President S R Nathan receiving a painting from a student from the Down Syndrome Association (DSA) of Singapore at the launch of Temasek Polytechnic (TP)'s 15th Anniversary Celebrations in February 2005. Source: Ministry of Information, Communications and the Arts Collection, courtesy of the National Archives of Singapore. Reprinted with permission.

President S R Nathan accompanied by the Yang Di-Pertuan Agong of Malaysia Tuanku Syed Sirajuddin after attending the official welcoming ceremony upon arrival in Kuala Lumpur for a five-day State Visit to Malaysia from April 11 to 15, 2005. Source: Ministry of Information, Communications and the Arts Collection, courtesy of the National Archives of Singapore. Reprinted with permission.

President and NTU Chancellor S R Nathan (seated centre) with Senior Minister Goh Chok Tong (seated right) at a dinner with former Indian President Dr Abdul Kalam (seated left), NTU's senior management, and other distinguished guests on the occasion of Dr Kalam being awarded the degree of Doctor of Engineering (*honoris causa*) in August 2008. Picture courtesy of the Nathan Family.

President and Mrs S R Nathan visiting the Marina Barrage in 2009. Source: Ministry of Information, Communications and the Arts Collection, courtesy of the National Archives of Singapore. Reprinted with permission.

President and Mrs S R Nathan officiating at the Outstanding Social Worker Award Ceremony held at the Istana in 2010. Source: Ministry of Information, Communications and the Arts Collection, courtesy of the National Archives of Singapore. Reprinted with permission.

President S R Nathan with Chairman Gerard Ee and National Kidney Foundation's (NKF) Chief Executive Officer Mrs Eunice Tay displaying the calligraphy piece President Nathan did to raise funds at the auction during NKF's charity dinner at Grand Ballroom, Orchid Country Club in 2011. The Chinese characters "ren ai" (仁爱) mean benevolence. Source: Ministry of Information, Communications and the Arts Collection, courtesy of the National Archives of Singapore. Reprinted with permission.

Mr Nathan, a Mentor for All Seasons

Mr S R Nathan (first from left) with Mr S Chandra Das (third from left), Singapore's Trade Representative in Moscow, and two security officers during PM Lee Kuan Yew's trip to the Soviet Union in October 1970. Picture courtesy of Mr S Chandra Das.

Mr S R Nathan, Director, SID, with Mr Eddie Teo on a visit to Milford Sound, New Zealand, in 1972. Mr Teo is currently the Chairman of the Public Service Commission as well as Chairman of the RSIS Board of Governors. Picture courtesy of Mr Eddie Teo.

Mr S R Nathan with members of the Inter-Religious Organisation, Singapore (IRO) at the Katho Chengsia Temple in August 1999. Source: Ministry of Information, Communications and the Arts Collection, courtesy of the National Archives of Singapore. Reprinted with permission.

President S R Nathan with RSIS Dean, Ambassador Barry Desker, and RSIS graduates at NTU's 2008 Convocation Ceremony.

Visit by RSIS staff to the Istana, by invitation of President S R Nathan, April 17, 2009. Picture from Associate Professor Kumar Ramakrishna's personal collection.

President S R Nathan with guests from Deutsche Bank — donor for the Singapore International Foundation's Water for Life project, Siem Reap, Cambodia, at the SIF Partner for Good Appreciation Dinner 2010. Picture courtesy of the Singapore International Foundation.

President S R Nathan with former colleagues from the Singapore Press Holdings at the Istana in January 2011. Picture courtesy of Mr Peter H L Lim.

Mr S R Nathan, High Commissioner of Singapore to Malaysia, treating the staff of the Singapore High Commission in Kuala Lumpur to a *makan kecil* (tea session), after a busy period of official activities. Picture from Ambassador Ong Keng Yong's personal collection.

Former MFA colleagues gathering for lunch with Mr S R Nathan at Hai Tien Lo, Pan Pacific Hotel, Singapore, in March 2016. Picture from Mr Mushahid Ali's personal collection.

Reflections: Foreign Service

The MFA Years
Barry Desker

Boss, Mentor, and Friend
Calvin Eu Mun Hoo

Calm and Cool Leader
A Selvarajah

S R Nathan: Mentor with Heart
Seetoh Hoy Cheng

S R Nathan: The Thought Leader
S Gopinath Pillai

The MFA Years

Barry Desker

For the first generation of MFA officers, S R Nathan was the key figure who shaped their perspectives on the Singapore Foreign Service and the role of the fledgling Ministry of Foreign Affairs. Joining the Ministry of Foreign Affairs (MFA) in February 1966 as an Assistant Secretary, he rose rapidly through the ranks of the Ministry and became Deputy Secretary (Political) in 1969. He became the 'go-to' person for the political leadership, diplomats posted to Singapore and a younger group of MFA officers nurtured by him.

I joined in April 1970 as part of an intake that year which provided the critical base for MFA in the 1980s and 1990s. Peter Chan, Tony Siddique, Lin Chung Ying, Edward Lee, Lee Yoke Kwang, and Michael Cheok were contemporaries. Mark Hong who had joined in late 1969 and Kishore Mahbubani from the 1971 batch were also associated with this group as they were the only survivors of their respective intakes. The 1970 cohort had as great an impact on MFA as the 1979 intake, whose representatives included Ong Keng Yong, A Selvarajah, Calvin Eu, Simon De Cruz, and Robert Chua. The striking feature is that for both groups, S R Nathan was their first boss, and his vision, perspectives, and approach to the making of Singapore foreign policy and the challenges facing Singapore shaped their thinking. Those who did not make the cut quickly fell by the wayside and moved on to other careers.

S R Nathan demanded crisp and sharply argued assessments, "cutting out all the palaver". The Prime Minister wanted the essence of the issue in two pages and this was what was provided, using Sir Ernest Gowers' *The Complete Plain Words* as the style book. For recent graduates trained in the social sciences, it required an adjustment in writing styles to focus on reaching the reader, not just winning the approval of academics.

Hosting CHOGM

Mr Nathan was a demanding boss. As Singapore was hosting the first Commonwealth Heads of Government Meeting (CHOGM) in January 1971, his inexperienced team of nine officers bore the brunt of responsibility for preparing the briefs for the meeting, working late into the night in the weeks leading to the meeting. One of the members (who did not stay long in MFA) was remiss in not destroying spoilt cyclostyled copies, as well as earlier drafts, and had piled them up next to the cyclostyling machine. Mr Nathan found these copies, and wanted to know who the culprit was, so that stiff disciplinary action could be taken for the security breach. The group decided that although it was caused by one of them, we would jointly take responsibility for the error. Mr Nathan was unhappy and threatened a full security investigation, but admitted later that it showed that a sense of camaraderie was developing.

Mr Nathan moved to the Ministry of Home Affairs shortly thereafter, and became Director of the Security and Intelligence Division of the Ministry of Defence in August 1971. During the years thereafter, MFA stagnated. MFA was barely coping with issues handled by the Ministry. It attracted a mixed bag of recruits each year who were often attracted by the glamour of diplomacy rather than any real interest in foreign policy issues. The overall performance of the Ministry was third-rate. Mr Nathan returned to MFA as First Permanent Secretary in February 1979 after the Vietnamese invasion and occupation of Cambodia in December 1978. Singapore was facing its greatest foreign policy and security challenge, and Prime Minister Lee Kuan Yew had told Mr Nathan that he had two years to build up MFA or he would close down the Ministry and make it part of the Prime Minister's Department. Mr Nathan's task was to build up MFA so that it functioned as well as leading foreign services, such as the British diplomatic service.

Mr Nathan enjoyed a relationship of mutual respect and confidence with the Second Permanent Secretary, Chia Cheong Fook, who was a close personal friend dating from the time they started their careers in the social service sector in the 1950s. Mr Chia handled the administration of MFA. He brought in Jaya Mohideen from the Public Service Commission. She worked closely with the two permanent secretaries in recruitment and training to build up the Foreign Service. Stellar appointments included the 1979 batch, and Bilahari

Kausikan who joined in 1981 and eventually rose to become Permanent Secretary. Lee Chiong Giam was appointed as Director (Regional and Economic) and See Chak Mun returned from Canberra as Director (Political) after serving as the first professional MFA officer to be appointed as an ambassador.

Revamping MFA

In 1979, Mr Nathan started the circulation of 'Information Notes' containing one- to two-page assessments. The first 'Information Notes' on China's invasion of Vietnam were issued by Mr Nathan with the Deputy Directors for International and Southeast Asia divisions. When the Iran/Iraq War began in September 1980, the Desk Officer Ong Keng Yong and the supervising Deputy Director Michael Cheok flooded the circulation list with quick, regular updates on developing trends in the conflict. Mr Nathan also established a Duty Office headed each week by Deputy Directors on a rotational basis after the Chinese 'lesson' to Vietnam in February 1979. The China desk staff had gone about their usual Sunday routines and had missed the reports of the Chinese retaliatory invasion of Vietnam. Mr Nathan was incensed. "You must be seized with the issues" was one of his favourite lines. His view was that country officers needed to be aware of breaking news developments whether they were in the office or enjoying a relaxing Sunday. MFA must not be caught out by unexpected developments, and the Duty Office should alert MFA senior staff immediately.

To keep senior officers briefed on rapidly changing developments, Mr Nathan instituted the practice of

'Morning Prayers' daily at 10.00 am. These meetings lasted for about half an hour, and the Directors and Deputy Directors would brief the meeting on breaking news covered by the Reuters, AFP and AP news agencies, as well as any information picked up by listening to shortwave radio broadcasts or reports from our overseas missions. Mr Nathan would provide directions on follow-up action. The result was a Ministry whose key officers could respond coherently when approached for reactions to the latest developments. Mr Nathan was harsh in criticising the officers' assessment of the implications of issues raised in their presentations. Once a week, a desk officer would be selected to brief the 'Morning Prayers'. This meant that Mr Nathan could quickly assess whether the officer understood issues within his area of responsibility and grasped Singapore's concerns or was just 'dead wood'.

Policy Shift

Mr Nathan also instituted a fundamental staffing policy shift. The most senior capable officers were assigned to MFA headquarters. The best of the 1979 batch of officers had their postings delayed. The effect was that MFA's performance in terms of meeting the requirements of the Prime Minister improved considerably. MFA staff were also taken more seriously in inter-Ministry interactions because there was no longer a revolving door where MFA seemed to be represented by different officers at each meeting because of the policy of posting senior officers to overseas missions. Over time, foreign ambassadors based in Singapore started dealing with MFA directors and deputy directors as they were able to obtain answers and did not have to await a meeting with the Minister or Permanent Secretary.

Given Singapore's location, Mr Nathan was always focused on Singapore's two neighbours, Malaysia and Indonesia. He was willing to put MFA's best analysts on these desks, ensuring that some of our top officers were posted to these embassies, and began the practice of training officers in specialised area studies accompanied by language training.

The terms and conditions of service were also improved in these more difficult embassies, as MFA had previously prioritised the cost of living allowances and benefits for staff serving in what were deemed the more expensive postings like New York, London or Paris. As someone whose first job in MFA was that of Malaysia Desk Officer in 1970, taking over as Head of the Southeast Asia division in 1971 (with staff who were all older than me), and having gone on a Ford Fellowship from 1972 to 1974 for my Masters' degree on no-pay leave to specialise on Southeast Asia, especially Indonesia, followed by a posting as Counsellor in Jakarta, I was a beneficiary of this shift in policy.

International Diplomacy

As the aftermath of Vietnam's invasion and occupation of Cambodia took centre stage in Singapore's international diplomacy, Mr Nathan instituted measures to build up MFA's capabilities in international negotiations and lobbying. Following the setback at the Non-Aligned Summit in Havana in September 1979, where the Democratic Kampuchea (DK) delegation was blocked by the Cuban hosts from taking its seat and a vacant seat declared, Mr Nathan met Tony Siddique and me just before we left for New York to attend the 34th United Nations (UN) General Assembly. He was clear that Singapore would be facing a major challenge in ensuring that the DK delegation continued to represent Cambodia, and that there would be a need for strong backing for the resolution which the ASEAN states would be sponsoring.

The message was that this was the primary focus of our role at the coming UN General Assembly session. Mr Nathan harboured no illusions and was adamant that this was the only standard of judgement for the performance of the UN team that year. (To complete the picture, India proposed an amendment to the Report of the Credentials Committee at the UN General Assembly calling for a vacant seat to be declared, taking its cue from the Cuban decision in Havana. Instead of the amendment being voted on first, Ambassador Tommy Koh had to argue that the Indian proposal was not an amendment, but a completely new resolution which should only be taken up after the vote on the Report. The outcome was very encouraging: 71 voted in favour of the adoption of the Committee's report, 35 against, 34 abstained, and 12 did not participate in the vote. This decision was followed by intensive lobbying in the following weeks to win support for the ASEAN position. The ASEAN-sponsored resolution was eventually adopted by 91 votes to 21 against, with 29 abstentions.

MFA's Coming of Age

The Cambodian issue was a coming of age for the Ministry of Foreign Affairs. The Minister for Foreign Affairs,

Mr S. Rajaratnam, provided the intellectual leadership and spoke articulately at ASEAN meetings, Non-Aligned Summits and Ministerial Meetings and at the UN General Assembly. However, S R Nathan, as the First Permanent Secretary, played a key role in institution building, nurturing a band of politically alert and operationally skilled multilateral diplomats. When the Prime Minister Lee Kuan Yew mentioned to the United States Permanent Representative to the UN Jeane Kirkpatrick during her visit to Singapore in May 1984 that the Singapore foreign service was like a DC3, slow and reliable, she responded that she thought that Singapore diplomats were more like F16s!

Mr Nathan played a critical role in facilitating the formation of the Cambodian coalition government in 1980–1981. He met Son Sann of the Khmer People's National Liberation Front (KPNLF), In Tam, the Special Envoy of Prince Sihanouk and Khieu Samphan of the Khmer Rouge during their September 1981 visit to Singapore. Mr Nathan told MFA officers that despite their show of bravado when talking about Sihanouk, Son Sann and Khieu Samphan acted submissively in Sihanouk's presence, they crawled to meet Sihanouk. He learnt from his interactions with Prince Sihanouk that Sihanouk saw himself as above the three factions and not as part of any of them. This recognition helped to shape MFA's interactions with the three Khmer factions as we had earlier leaned more in favour of Son Sann and the KPNLF.

For young MFA officers, the informal learning opportunities often had as great an impact as the formal interactions at meetings or when we were called to see him. He was well known for writing 'Please speak' when he wished to reprimand you or raise a point of clarification. While some of my colleagues went to see him every time there was such a note, others checked with his secretary what his mood was before venturing to meet him. Some like Tony Siddique would keep the file for a few days. If Mr Nathan did not say anything again, Tony would leave a note 'Spoken' next to Mr Nathan's query and file the document away!

We learnt informally through discussions over meals when we travelled to conferences and meetings or if, like Calvin Eu, we joined him for his morning walks. Mr Nathan would discuss his experiences at the Conference of the Afro-Asian People's Solidarity Organisation in Algiers in 1964, the early days in MFA when a North Korean visitor who was the equivalent of the Director of the Asian Division was treated as a state guest as he was introduced as the Vice-President of the Democratic People's Republic of Korea (DPRK) and Special Envoy of President Kim Il Sung, the atmospherics during the 1967 meeting in Bangkok which led to the formation of ASEAN, and the points to bear in mind in dealing with the requirements of the Prime Minister and other political leaders.

Even after he left MFA, Mr Nathan kept up his ties with those who had worked closely with him. We met from time to time over lunch when he was in *The Straits Times*. When he was appointed as High Commissioner to Malaysia, he would insist that his former colleagues stay with him if they were visiting Kuala Lumpur, just as he would host lunch or dinner if our paths took us to Washington when he was Ambassador to the United States. He continued to meet us even after he took office as the sixth President of Singapore.

My final memory of Mr Nathan was at a lunch to commemorate the 20th anniversary of the formation of the Institute of Defence and Strategic Studies (IDSS) on July 28, 2016. He had a very relaxed exchange with those of us present. After the lunch, he wrote a personal note to each of those present at the lunch. In his note to me, among others, he mentioned our relationship over 45 years. "To have stuck together, through thick and thin and [maintained] this close friendship speaks much about the purpose we all share in our life time. Thank you ever so much for the friendship, faith and support you ungrudgingly gave me. Comradery marked our life and so I hope it will be for the rest of our years."

Ambassador Barry Desker *is a Distinguished Fellow and former Dean of the S. Rajaratnam School of International Studies. Ambassador Desker previously worked with Mr S R Nathan at the Ministry of Foreign Affairs. He is also currently Non-Resident Ambassador to the Holy See and Spain.*

Boss, Mentor, and Friend

Calvin Eu Mun Hoo

The late Mr S R Nathan recruited me into MFA in June 1979 when he was then the first Permanent Secretary. He was the boss who demanded exacting standards, and sharply focused, crisp, and succinct analysis and writing. He was always firm with a bracing bluntness, but fair. Over the years, I have learnt that he was actually helping me to realise my full potential. I was fortunate that he became my mentor who patiently shared his vast wisdom and deep knowledge with me, and accepted me as a friend despite the wide difference in our ages. Notwithstanding my relatively short stint in MFA HQ, he had consistently tracked and shaped my entire 35-year career in MFA, for which I will forever be indebted. His dedication, commitment, and relentless pursuit of excellence will always inspire MFA officers of my generation.

A few weeks into my job, Mr Nathan summoned me for an interview. He pointed out that my immediate superiors had failed to assign me more serious work, and that bred restlessness which would certainly provide me the excuse for my resignation. He swiftly assigned me as an area specialist on Indonesia and simultaneously placed me on the international/regional conference circuit.

That interview essentially placed me on orders, which initiated the heavy demands on me and hard work to come. Soon, I was on numerous diplomatic courier duties to Medan and Jakarta, with the additional task to build a network of contacts in Indonesia as well as to observe and imbibe their sociocultural ethos and language. These exposures facilitated an easy breaking-in period when I was posted to Jakarta in July 1981.

In addition to manning the desk, I was appointed as a 'resource' person on matters related to the Straits of Malacca, and subsequently to ABRI, the Indonesian Armed Forces. As 'conference-goer', I was the designated secretary tasked to handle all the substantive as well as administrative requirements of the delegation. The tasks were both physically and intellectually taxing. There were numerous and frequent overseas trips, but the more significant ones were then PM Lee Kuan Yew's official visit to Indonesia (July 1980), as well as for the inauguration of Philippine President Marcos in Manila in June 1981, preceded by a private visit to Taiwan. These were enriching experiences for a rookie like me, particularly in preparing the briefs for and taking notes during the visits, but they took a toll on my personal life. Eventually, I was compelled, albeit with low expectation, to request to be 'grounded' so that I could marry, settle down, and start a family. After some thought and with a smile, Mr Nathan reluctantly agreed to post me to Jakarta on condition that I got married first. While he preferred that I should remain in MFA to hone my skills, he believed that it would be better to stabilise myself and start a family. I was pleasantly surprised that beneath his titanium mask, Mr Nathan had a huge degree of empathy. Hence, I was the first of the 1979 cohort to be posted overseas after having served about two years in HQ.

As a professional, Mr Nathan demanded analytical rigour in policy planning and implementation. It was a given for each policy input to be well formulated and buttressed on strong intellectual arguments. He would growl if 'updating' a brief was a cavalier act of merely adding more information without excising the outdated ones. In his view, a voluminous brief only epitomised a bankruptcy of thought, lacking clarity and incisive recommendations. In the pursuit of excellence, he meted out harsh treatment on my immediate superiors in the briefs' preparations and policy submissions. Files would be thrown and drafts torn to bits before us. He even threatened them: "If you cannot handle the job, let Calvin take over yours!" That threat etched a deep impression on a recruit like me. It demonstrated his steadfast commitment in making significant contributions to our foreign policy process and demanding each to give his best.

After a couple of months on the desk, I had my first direct and personal encounter in working with Mr Nathan on a brief on Indonesia (September 1979), an area where he had an enduring interest and deep insights. We had robust exchanges in identifying and defining the objectives and interests of the visit (I was fortunate to have the support of Mr Barry Desker, then Counsellor in our Embassy in Jakarta, in drafting the first cut of the brief).

In that exercise, Mr Nathan required me to explain the 'whats' and 'whys' of the brief, who were its consumers, and how we would assist them to achieve the stated objectives and/or interests. These were the tenets of a quality brief that must be crisp and succinctly written too. On the surface, they seemed basic even bordering on being simplistic. In reality, they were extremely challenging to achieve if one lacked the depth and knowledge of the subjects and their preoccupations. My brief writing exercise with Mr Nathan was my very first in MFA, and it was more than a '101' course. That momentous experience was embedded in me throughout my entire career.

In my pre-posting departure call on Mr Nathan, he imparted another key enduring lesson to me. Recalling his experience from the Laju incident, he highlighted the virtue of staying calm and collected particularly during a crisis. That would allow one to think through the issue and various alternative courses of action. Anxiety would only generate more panic, resulting in clouded analyses and poor judgment calls. He added that a senior officer should be the shield against the mounting pressure from the upper echelon so as to allow the desk and missions time to assess the issues and formulate the solutions. Impulsive action and/or reaction would result in a disastrous policy. I have faithfully followed this valuable principle throughout my career in MFA, where crises erupted frequently, with some sustained for protracted periods.

Mr Nathan left MFA to head The Straits Times Press while I was still serving in Jakarta. On my return to MFA following my post-graduate studies on a Fulbright scholarship in the United States (1986), he would regularly invite me to one-on-one meals where he would enquire about my work, family, and discuss developments in Southeast Asia, ASEAN, as well as a variety of regional issues. When I was the Ambassador in Thailand and Republic of Korea, and High Commissioner in India, Mr Nathan was the President, and he would plan private vacations in these countries where my wife and I would be included as part of his extended family. (He made a state visit to the ROK in April 2002). Throughout these memorable encounters, I was more an apprentice tapping his reservoir of distilled knowledge and wisdom, which he patiently and willingly shared with me. He unfailingly maintained our friendship and communication link till his passing on August 22, 2016.

Mr Nathan will always be my source of inspiration. As a recruit, he had put me through a crucible that had steeled me both in strength, confidence, and knowledge. I have gained immensely from his valuable guidance and wisdom. I will greatly miss my boss, mentor, and friend. I will try imparting what he had taught me to our younger generations of MFA officers.

***Mr Calvin Eu** is an Adjunct Senior Fellow at the S. Rajaratnam School of International Studies. Mr Eu previously worked with Mr S R Nathan at the Ministry of Foreign Affairs, during which, he served in several Ambassadorial positions.*

Calm and Cool Leader

A Selvarajah

I first met Mr S R Nathan when I joined MFA in July 1979. He was appointed as Permanent Secretary of MFA only a few months earlier. He had come with instructions from then Prime Minister Mr Lee Kuan Yew to improve the work of MFA. I was one of the young officers who were appointed as Secretary to the weekly management meetings, which Mr Nathan chaired. He also started daily morning briefings for the PS, which is now known as 'morning prayers'. The other initiatives that Mr Nathan introduced were the Duty Office and Information Notes. These are all his legacies to MFA.

As Secretary to the weekly management meetings, which usually lasted from about 9.00am to 12.30pm, at which Polar curry puffs and *vadai* were usually served, with the help of another MFA institution, Mr Sanasi, I had the opportunity to observe how Mr Nathan managed the Ministry. Mr Nathan ran the Ministry with a lot of common sense that he gained from his life experience, time spent in the civil service, and with a good understanding of what our first generation leaders Mr Lee Kuan Yew, Dr Goh Keng Swee, and Mr S. Rajaratnam stood for and expected from their civil servants. I remember Mr Nathan telling me: "Once you have worked for Dr Goh, you are never the same again." Once in Washington DC, serving as his DCM, I asked Mr Nathan, I cannot remember exactly on what issue, why Mr Lee was taking this position. Mr Nathan also seemed puzzled, but he replied: "Selva, you and I can only look three years ahead for Singapore, but Mr Lee thinks 50 years ahead. So we do not have the capacity to understand his reasoning", and we then went about dutifully carrying out the instruction. As the Secretary of the weekly meeting, I also observed how Mr Nathan used the meetings to ensure that matters discussed were followed through and that lapses that occurred in MFA were rectified and not repeated again. Mr Nathan's famous remarks on files were 'Please speak'. When you received a file with the words 'Please speak', you often wondered whether you were asked to come in for a discussion or a good scolding. Those times watching how Mr Nathan ran the Ministry was a good learning experience for me and my colleagues as young officers. Mr Nathan would tell us to make the briefs tight and concise. His famous words were "cut off the palaver and keep it crisp".

After Mr Nathan left MFA as Permanent Secretary in the early 1980s, I did not expect to work for him again. However, about 15 years later, I served as his DCM in Washington DC. While I was happy to take up the challenge of a posting in Washington DC, I went to Washington with some apprehension as I knew that Mr Nathan was a tough task master and would have high expectations of his Deputy. To add to my predicament, our worst bilateral crisis with the US, the Michael Fay episode, broke out a week after I assumed post in Washington. It was indeed a trying time for Mr Nathan and the Mission in Washington to handle the crisis. Fortunately, Mr Nathan provided calm and cool leadership, which made the challenge of handling the crisis easier for me and my colleagues. While he was aware that the Mission was working 16 hours daily during the crisis, he would never tell us not to work hard. However, in his own way, he would take care of our welfare by asking us what we were doing for lunch, and take us to a meal from time to time. It was his way of telling us, *I know that you chaps are working hard and under a lot of stress*. Watching how Mr Nathan handled the Larry King interview also taught me and my colleagues something about how to keep your cool and stand your ground when posed tough questions by the media.

Despite my initial apprehensions, I enjoyed my two years working with Mr Nathan in Washington. I discovered that he was demanding as a boss, but once he realised that you were responsible, hardworking, and can be trusted to carry out your duties without supervision, he gave you a lot of leeway to get your job done. It was a good learning experience for me following Mr Nathan to his meetings in the White House, Capitol Hill, and various United States Government Departments, and watching how he dealt with his interlocutors. Mr Nathan gave us broad directions and did not micromanage us, and trusted us to get the job done to the best of our ability. His only advice to me was that "if a job needs to be done, let us ensure that it is done to the best of our ability, and that is all that can be expected of us". After Mr Nathan, I was indeed fortunate to have another wonderful person,

Professor Chan Heng Chee, as my boss. Though both of them had different styles of working, I benefitted immensely from working as their Deputy and learning from them how a Head of Mission should carry out his duties.

Even after he left Washington and became Director of IDSS and later President of Singapore, Mr Nathan would send me goodies from Singapore by the diplomatic bag during my postings in Brussels and Berlin. Occasionally, he would send me a book which he felt would be useful for me to read. I also made it a point to reciprocate his kindness by sending him some goodies from Belgium and Germany.

Ambassador A Selvarajah *is currently Singapore's Ambassador to the Republic of Turkey. Ambassador Selvarajah previously worked with Mr S R Nathan at the Ministry of Foreign Affairs.*

S R Nathan: Mentor with Heart

Seetoh Hoy Cheng

Many accounts have been written by the first generation MFA officers of the 1960s and 1970s about the hot house tempering they underwent in the fledgling ministry, in particular by the late Mr S R Nathan. He was first Director, Political and Deputy Secretary between 1968 and 1971, and then returned as First Permanent Secretary in January 1979 until his retirement in 1982. I was among the Foreign Service Officers who were moulded as professionals during his second stint, as First Permanent Secretary (1PS).

I was assigned to the Political Division from the Administration Division in 1978. Some two months later, all the officers of the Political Division were summoned to the Prime Minister's Office at the Istana, where Prime Minister (PM) Lee Kuan Yew proceeded to give us a dressing down for 90 minutes. He upbraided us for not providing policy briefs, notes, and biographical data of visiting dignitaries of the requisite standard. One senior officer was severely taken to task for a lapse of common sense!

A few months later, in early 1979, Mr S R Nathan joined the Ministry of Foreign Affairs as Permanent Secretary (PS) with his predecessor, Mr Chia Cheong Fook, continuing as Second Permanent Secretary (2PS). His arrival at the Ministry a few months after PM's strictures to us meant that Mr Nathan was tasked with making sure that we performed up to PM's expectations. Mr Nathan set about reforming the way MFA Political Division worked and "beat" the officers into shape. Initially, he was tough on the senior officers for not giving the desk officers the requisite guidance; later, he gave his personal guidance to the younger officers, particularly those who were recruited by MFA in 1979.

I had the benefit of Mr Nathan's tutelage while working at the International Organisations and Third World desk. While covering the China desk for two officers who were overseas, I had to help prepare a brief on China for PM as a Chinese dignitary was making a visit to Singapore. The desk officer concerned had left me a partially prepared brief which I completed and sent up to Mr Nathan for clearance. Two days after I sent the draft brief to him, I was asked to see him with a copy of the draft brief. That came as a surprise, for it was not usual for Permanent Secretaries to see desk officers. Mr Nathan went through the draft brief with me, page by page. He asked me where I obtained this fact or that figure. Fortunately, I remembered the sources of information. Mr Nathan needed to know the source to assess the reliability of the information. He also amended loose and ambiguous statements. Since then, I made it a point to note the sources of information that were used for each fact or figure, and to be more precise in the construction of sentences in documents.

Following the invasion of Cambodia by Vietnam in December 1978 and the subsequent invasion of Vietnam by China in February 1979, there was a flurry of calls by foreign ambassadors on Minister and on PS separately. I was note-taker for several meetings. After the invasion of Afghanistan by the Soviet Union in December 1979, the US Ambassador called on Minister and PS separately to discuss the situation. Again, I was the note-taker and I learned a lot from the meetings. After one meeting with an Ambassador discussing the invasion of Vietnam, Mr Nathan told me that if he asked the Ambassador for the number of troops massed on the border, it did not mean he did not hear the number, but that he wanted me to record the number. He was helpful in that regard.

After I had reviewed past notes of conversations that were mainly two- to three-page documents prepared in double spacing that gave a summary of the discussions but did not reveal much to readers, I resolved to write more detailed notes of meeting. Once, after a long meeting between an Ambassador and PS, I sent the draft notes of the meeting to PS for clearance. He vetted the draft and returned the document to me with the remark, 'a good record'. It was encouraging and it motivated me to write better notes.

Mr Nathan introduced the daily morning meetings in the Ministry, where the desk officers would brief him on significant developments in the countries under their purview. Though the information was usually gleaned from the wire services (such as Reuters and AFP) that the Ministry subscribed to, we could learn a lot from the discussions that followed. Sometimes my colleagues found them dreadful when they could not answer the questions PS posed to them.

Mr Nathan also introduced the circulation of 'Information Notes' on current events, to train the officers to write analytical pieces clearly. He assigned the topics. The first topic he gave me for an 'Information Note' was on the Black groups opposing the white regime in Southern Rhodesia, now Zimbabwe. Mr Nathan required us to indicate on the 'Information Note', the names of the officers who prepared and cleared it. This was to ensure someone would be responsible for the accuracy of the facts. The date of preparation was also stated. So was the sign to show the end of the document. Mr Nathan would be riled if he saw a document without all these indications. He did not tolerate sloppy work. He would reprimand lazy officers and tell them hard work never killed anybody.

Mr Nathan also required desk officers to present roundups of developments in the countries and the performance of the overseas mission under their purview in fortnightly meetings chaired by him. This gave opportunities for officers to show their grasp of the issues pertaining to the countries in their desk. Speaking and analytical skills were developed. The supervisor was expected to help the desk officer prepare a good presentation.

The desk officer had the task of making written submissions to the PS on issues of concern, with recommendations for his approval. Sometimes, PS would send the file back to the desk officer with the words 'Please speak' written on the minute. I received a few of those requests. Mr Nathan had a very good memory. It was futile to hope that he would forget. It was best to go up and see him with the file, not knowing whether he was going to reprimand you or if he was seeking some clarification before deciding on a course of action. Asking the officer to speak also enabled Mr Nathan to get to know many officers in the Political Division and the Regional and Economic Division. He knew their strengths and weaknesses.

While Mr Nathan worked the officers hard, he also rewarded them. In September 1979, PS sent 2PS, Mr Chia Cheong Fook, Director of Regional and Economic Division (D/R+E), Lee Chiong Giam and me on an inspection visit to Bonn, Paris, Brussels, London, Moscow, Cairo, New Delhi and Bangkok. D/R+E told me my task was to take the notes of the conversations in all the meetings and he would write the report of the visits. 2PS who would 'do the talking in the meetings', when meeting with Foreign Ministry officials in each capital city we visited. I took more than 20 sets of notes for these meetings. Except for India, none of the countries we visited came under my purview. However, I learnt a lot in that trip. It was Mr Nathan's way of rewarding and providing on-the-job training for the officer. On my return, he asked me about the trip. I told him that it was good, but the Russians in Moscow never smiled. Mr Nathan said that they had nothing to smile about.

In early 1980, Mr Nathan told me that he would send me to Australia for the Australian Foreign Service Course, held from April to June. He said that it would be good for me. Although the Ministry was shorthanded, Mr Nathan was willing to send officers for training. The Australian Foreign Service course, which included lectures on international law, international economics, participation in mock conferences, and the opportunities to make off-the-cuff remarks was useful. Mr Nathan also sent the desk officers recruited in 1979 to short courses or master degree courses overseas to broaden their training.

When dignitaries from South Asia and Africa called on PM Lee Kuan Yew, Mr Nathan gave me the opportunity to take notes at those meetings. The *curriculum vitae* of the note-taker was sent to the Prime Minister's Office a few days in advance of the meeting. I recalled the meeting of the Commonwealth Secretary-General with PM Lee. They discussed the preparations for the Commonwealth Heads of Government Regional Meeting (CHOGRM) held in New Delhi in September 1980.

Mr Nathan included me in PM Lee's delegation to attend the CHOGRM held in New Delhi in September 1980. CHOGRM which alternated with the Commonwealth Heads of Government Meeting (CHOGM) subsequently lost its purpose and ended. Director of Political Division, See Chak Mun and I flew to New Delhi one day ahead of PM Lee's arrival, to see to the preparations. We checked PM's hotel room and other facilities. In New Delhi, I took notes of Minister Dhanabalan's meeting with India's External Affairs Minister at the Indian Ministry of External Affairs. From that visit to New Delhi to attend CHOGRM, I learnt what to do during PM Lee's visit.

In late 1980, Mr Nathan told me that he wanted to send me overseas to do a master's degree course, but the Public Service Commission (PSC) would not give such scholarships to female officers. He said that he would assign me to the Singapore Embassy in Washington, DC, so that I could pursue a post-graduate course part-time. He advised me not to embark on the course immediately on arrival, otherwise the ambassador would be unhappy. I was touched by his thoughtfulness and kindness. The Ministry created a new post in the Embassy in Washington, DC for my assignment to the post.

Before I left for Washington, DC in February 1981, 2PS met me. He told me that Mr Nathan had asked him to inform me that he would give me a promotion and that he would ask Director of Political Division to write my staff confidential report instead of the usual practice of my immediate supervisor writing my report. I received my promotion in April 1981. I learnt that Mr Nathan went to the promotion interview at the PSC.

One day in Washington, DC, I received a letter from Mr Nathan informing me that he was leaving MFA. He need not inform me that he was leaving the Ministry, but he did. It was so thoughtful of him. In those days, there was no circular minute to inform the staff of changes in the Ministry's organisation. There was no internet or e-mail in the Ministry then.

In three short years, Mr Nathan as Permanent Secretary transformed the Ministry of Foreign Affairs in the way we worked and dealt with crisis. He also showed that he cared for the officers' welfare and development. The

Ministry continues with the morning meetings, review of the work of overseas missions, preparation of Information Notes and the enhanced quality of issue and country briefs initiated by Mr Nathan. His training and mentoring stood me in good stead.

Ms Seetoh Hoy Cheng *previously worked with Mr S R Nathan at the Ministry of Foreign Affairs, during which she served in several Ambassadorial positions.*

S R Nathan: The Thought Leader

S Gopinath Pillai

Much has been spoken and written about Mr Nathan's achievements, but not much attention has been given to the very strong views he had on many issues. In this short essay, I would look at his views on two important subjects, namely Singapore's foreign relations and Singapore's domestic situation. I recall telling a foreign ambassador some two decades ago that Mr S R Nathan was the most influential Indian in Singapore. To his incredulous query as to how I came to that conclusion, I told him as follows — in Singapore, there were people who were very influential with the grassroots. They read the ground well and they were effective dealing with the grassroots leaders. Then there were others who had strong links with top government leaders. Mr Nathan was one with strong links to both the grassroots as well as top leadership. His links with grassroots was not only restricted to the Indian community, but cut across all communities. Hence, my conclusion that he was a very influential person. I also disabused the Ambassador of his notion that civil servants are not influential. In Singapore, they certainly were.

I have narrated this episode here only to underscore the point that while Mr Nathan's achievements were inspirational, he was also a thoughtful person whose views on important issues needed to be studied.

Singapore's Foreign Relations

There are two documents that give an insight on what Mr Nathan saw as the foundation of Singapore's foreign policy. The first document is the inaugural S. Rajaratnam Lecture President Nathan delivered to the MFA Academy in March 2008. In this, he quotes from Mr Rajaratnam's speech in September 1965 when Singapore became member of the UN, and he explains how Singapore sees itself as a non-aligned country. Mr Rajaratnam says: "This does not mean that Singapore equates non-alignment with indifference to basic issues of right and wrong or that it will evade taking a stand on matters it considers vital lest it displeases some member nations including those with which it has close ties."

The second document is Mr Nathan's conversation with Timothy Auger in 2015, where he quotes from Mr Lee Kuan Yew's speech in 2009, as follows: "A small country must seek a maximum number of friends, while maintaining the freedom to be itself as a sovereign and independent nation. Both parts of the equation — a maximum number of friends and freedom to be ourselves — are equally important and inter-related" (Nathan 2015, 46).

Mr Nathan's views on Singapore's foreign policy are significantly influenced by both Mr Lee and Mr Rajaratnam.

Mr Nathan sees four trends that will affect international relations. These are globalisation, the evolving strategic framework in Asia, global terrorism, and non-traditional security challenges such as climate change, environmental degradation, and competition for resources. He felt that diplomacy was going to be conducted differently, and the diplomats handling this needed to be trained differently and they need to be equipped with a greater armoury of skills while being realistic and understood our limitations.

He felt the rise of China raised serious issues that needed to be handled carefully. Unlike other major Asian countries like Japan, India, and Indonesia, China wanted to extend its influence beyond its neighbourhood, seeking a significant role in regional and global matters. This would inevitably lead to rivalry between the United States and China. The tone and content of his speeches and writings seem to indicate that he is troubled by the prospects of dealing with this situation. He was not unhappy by the rise of China *per se* because he saw it as inevitable considering China's rapid economic growth. He wanted to ensure that Singapore, which is deft at handling the United States and the EU, will have the same dexterity in handling an assertive rising China.

I have asked myself what his reaction would have been on the current state of Singapore–China relations if he was around now. My view is that he would feel that while country to country relationship would be sorted out over time with what he terms 'quiet diplomacy', the damage done by the vitriolic comments on social media, which would have caused him considerable sadness may take longer to mend.

Apart from his thoughts on Singapore's foreign policy at the macro level which he expressed freely, Mr Nathan was always ready to advise diplomats who faced issues that needed to be handled diplomatically. On a personal level, I once sought his advice when I was High Commissioner to Pakistan. After having served about seven years, during which time I had developed excellent relations with senior Pakistani officials, I was asked during one of my representational visits why, as a businessman, I did not consider investing in Pakistan as I had done in India. I told the official who posed this question that, as a matter of principle, I do not invest in a country where I was the official representative of my country.

I narrated this story to Mr Nathan. He told me that I should not take this as a casual conversation. He said the Pakistanis may have been feeling uncomfortable with my Indian investments and hence, my effectiveness as Singapore's High Commissioner would be reduced. I felt he was right and decided to step down from my position. I could give many more anecdotes of the experience of other diplomats with Mr Nathan.

Singapore's Domestic Situation

Mr Nathan was proud of the fact in its short history Singapore has succeeded in creating a strong identity which highlighted individual cultures — Chinese, Malay, Indian, and more — but at the same time, created a Singaporean brand. He felt a small country like Singapore was particularly vulnerable to social and political instability and hence, policies implemented must help to stabilise the domestic situation. It was this fundamental concern that informed his guidance and leadership of the various communities, in the words of the National Pledge, to be one united people regardless of race, language, or religion.

In his conversation with Timothy Auger, he seemed more than a little concerned at the way the Singaporean society was evolving. He sees persistent expression of dissatisfaction, rising intolerance, commercial evangelism, the desire to flaunt wealth, and the weakening of the bond that existed between the government and the people on which modern Singapore was built as some of his concerns. He serves this warning: "Those who think that steering the ship is an easy matter or that it can be done by anyone should pause for thought and ask themselves if they might be wrong. Given our circumstances one or two wrong turns in social or economic policies could easily lead to problems that prove insoluble" (Nathan 2015, 214).

When the Institute of South Asian Studies (ISAS) was set up, he asked me to look into the possibility of organising a conference of the South Asian diaspora. We worked on it and organised the first one in 2011. So far, we have had three which were all very successful. The last one was in July 2016. At this conference, we conferred the 'Outstanding Member of the South Asian Diaspora' on Mr Nathan. As he was in hospital, the award was received on his behalf by his grandchildren.

Mr Nathan was a thought leader who instinctively identified opportunities as well as pitfalls. Sometimes his criticisms can be scathing and his praises seldom generous, but what he says is well intentioned and we ignore it at our peril.

The legacy that Mr Nathan has left behind through his books and speeches is significant. It would be worthwhile for some of our think tanks to study them in depth.

Ambassador S Gopinath Pillai is currently Ambassador-at-Large, Ministry of Foreign Affairs. He has worked with Mr S R Nathan in various community organisations.

Reflections: Security and Intelligence

S R Nathan and His Leadership Role in the Laju Affair 1974
Tee Tua Ba

S R Nathan and His Leadership Role in the Laju Affair 1974

Tee Tua Ba

My first opportunity and privilege of working with Mr S R Nathan was in the 1974 Laju hijack when he was the Director of Security and Intelligence (MINDEF) and I was Officer-in-Charge, Marine Police. On January 31, 1974, four international terrorists attacked with explosives the Shell Oil Refinery on Pulau Bukom. In attempting to escape, the terrorists, comprising two members of the Popular Front for the Liberation of Palestine (PFLP) and two Japanese Red Army guerrillas, hijacked a Shell Company ferry boat known as Laju (Malay for 'fast') with a number of hostages. For eight days, Singapore was in a state of emergency as the Laju hijack seized headlines in newspapers locally and abroad.

Prior to the attack on Singapore, in 1972, the PFLP attacked the Olympic village in Munich and took several Israeli athletes hostage. The German Police operation went awry resulting in the killing of all the Palestinian terrorists and Israeli athletes.

As for the Japanese Red Army, they were responsible for the massacre of innocent victims at Lod Airport, Israel during the same period.

Police Response to Attack

It was past 11.00 am in the morning when my Duty Inspector rushed into my office and cried out: "Bukom is bombed. There is shooting and explosion on Pulau Bukom Shell Refinery and there are two or three armed men creating havoc…". The message for help from the auxiliary police from Pulau Bukom was vague. During the explosion, two Air Defence aircraft were coincidentally flying past on training, hence, some thought it was an aerial attack on Pulau Bukom. Nobody on the island including the officer-in-charge, Inspector Nonis, knew what was happening. Panic was everywhere. There was absolute chaos and confusion on Pulau Bukom.

No one, therefore, knew or was aware of the deeper implications of this episode and its sensitivity until the drama finally unfolded. When I was first alerted, I was under the impression that it was a straightforward serious criminal case involving armed robbers who could be pirates from our neighbouring offshore islands. I was worried that there might be casualties or people killed by the explosion or gun fire, and the most important thing on my mind was to get to the scene urgently. I then directed the Duty Inspector to contact Pulau Bukom police for further and more specific facts. Simultaneously, I marshalled all available officers and, in a few words, impressed upon them the urgency and seriousness of the situation. I then directed them to be fully armed and ready to move to Pulau Bukom.

As my speed craft approached Pulau Bukom, I could see a huge plume of black smoke curling in the air on the horizon, and radio message crying out: "Pulau Bukom is bombed... It is hijacked... Please stop... Marine Police, help...help", from Inspector Nonis of Bukom police. Very soon after, I could see a ferry passenger boat steaming on the horizon hotly pursued by two Marine police crafts. As stated, at that time I strongly suspected the armed hijackers could be pirates from the neighbouring islands. Whatever it was, it was clear to me that we could not allow the suspect hijacked ferry boat to get away. It then occurred to me that I might have to resort to the use of violent force to immobilise and stop the hijacked ferry boat. Confusion continued to prevail as the hot pursuit continued with more police craft joining in — all in all 10 police craft.

I then established command and took control of the situation. In order to avoid confusion over the radio communication network, I instructed Operations Room to put on the 'talk through' for me in the Command Boat PB30. Thereafter, command and control was effectively established.

In Hot Pursuit of Hijacked Ferry Boat

Whilst being pursued, the Laju suddenly turned and indicated its intention to head for international waters in the direction of the Indonesian island, Pulau Sambu. I could not allow the pirates to get away so blatantly, otherwise this would have adverse repercussions for shipping security in Singapore. I decided to give a warning and then to fire at the wheel-house of Laju in order to immobilise it. It then occurred to me that there could be innocent hostages on board. Despite the initial confusion over the radio set, the message finally came through that, indeed, there were hostages on board. I then instructed our men to lower their weapons and not to be provocative. No one was to open fire until I specifically gave the order. Subsequently, the order came over the air from Operations Command Marine HQ that I was to withhold fire as there were indeed several innocent hostages on board the Laju. In order to avoid attack from the Indonesian navy, I informed Operations Command to alert the Indonesian Embassy that we would be entering Indonesian territorial waters in pursuit of the hijacked ferry Laju.

Whilst the pursuit continued towards Indonesian territorial waters, the Laju, to our surprise, suddenly turned around and headed towards our harbour instead. The Laju possibly realised that it was useless to head for the open international waters and be isolated for the 'kill' in the open sea. It then began to head in the direction of our harbour where it could take cover in our busy shipping anchorage. As my Command Craft PB30 drew near the Laju, the hijackers waved their weapons threateningly and beckoned us to keep our distance. The Laju, which was quite big compared to our police craft, majestically entered our harbour. I instructed all pursuing police craft to form a tight cordon around the Laju. Two Maritime gunboats from our Navy then joined our cordon and the eight-day siege commenced. Suddenly, one of the hijackers began to wave to me and showed me a blue plastic container which I initially thought was plastic explosives. I then directed all our crafts to keep a safe distance. The hijacker then threw the container into the water and beckoned me to pick it up. I retrieved the container which was actually a plastic bottle containing a written message. The message, in English and in long hand, declared:

> ... We are Japanese Red Army and Popular Front for the Liberation of Palestine. Just now, we exploded the Pulau Bukom's tank for solidarity with Vietnamese revolutional people. And for making the revolutional situation after consideration of today's oil crisis.
>
> Now we want negotiation with you. Call at once, the Japanese Ambassador! Hostages are in our hand. And we have big explosives with us.
>
> If you let us carried to the airport we promise you never kill them. But if you try to attack us, we explode ourselves. We want escape to another country.

The politics of this had thrown an entirely different complexion upon the whole case. The full text therefore had to be rapidly and accurately relayed to Police High Command Operations Room. At the same time, to keep in direct contact and dialogue, I told the hijackers that I would be conveying their message to our Higher Authority and they should wait for our response. I realised early that this was no longer purely a police case, but one in which the Foreign Ministry, and possibly the Cabinet, would be involved in. I knew it would be a long drawn out affair and we would have to be prepared for a long siege.

The Siege and Standoff

Upon conveying the written message by the terrorists, I reiterated the call for the Japanese Ambassador.

However, it took a long time, and the hijackers were getting impatient, agitated and waving their hands and weapons in the air. I realised that unless a channel of direct communication was established with the hijackers, misunderstanding could trigger an ugly incident. The hijackers continued to be in a highly excitable state and were impatient for our response. They were suspicious of police presence. Whenever police boats came too near, they would gesticulate violently with their weapons and waved our boats away.

It was indeed a very tense situation. I was wondering why it took so long for Higher Command to respond upon receipt of such an important message and threatening demand from the Bukom hijackers. Upon full appraisal, I decided that the standoff situation could not continue as it could likely trigger an ugly incident, so I had to do something. I decided to communicate and establish direct contact by keeping up a dialogue and engage the hijackers. By then, the hijackers became aware that I was the officer in command as I was the one who retrieved their message. To indicate my approach, I stood on deck of PB30 Command Boat and waved my scarf to attract their attention as I slowly approached the Laju. I ordered all my men down in the bridge and to conceal their weapons. They would take hostile action only if the hijackers open fire at me.

I indicated my intention clearly to the hijackers that I would be approaching. They remained suspicious, watchful, and behind cover with their weapons on the ready as I approached. At first, they hesitated but I insisted on going nearer. They then conceded. I signalled that I was not armed and would like to talk to them. I was fully aware that I was not dealing with ordinary criminals or psychopaths who would react irrationally on impulse. I believed they were intelligent men who were fully aware of their situation. Being tightly cordoned, they would only be endangering their own lives if they were to shoot me. It was a calculated risk to establish direct contact, and that paid dividends later throughout the siege. It was through this method that I was able to enhance my role, as the ground commander and negotiator, when meeting them directly face to face to assess their reaction, develop confidence and trust in me as the spokesman of the Singapore Government. I was fully aware that in arrogating myself this role, the hijackers would be observing and assessing whatever I said and did to the minutest detail. There was no precedence to follow as we had never faced such a major well-organised international terrorist attack before, and I had to adapt my tactic in dealing directly with the situation.

My primary objective was to stabilise the situation while waiting for instructions from Higher Command, as it had escalated to more than purely a police case. I soon became the 'face' of the Singapore Government to the hijackers. It was through me that they assessed and gauged the reaction and response of the Singapore Government. I realised that this was a critical 'poker game' that I must play to win at all cost. Unknown to me, the Laju had a communication set which enabled them to communicate directly with Pulau Bukom. The hijackers were getting angry and very impatient waiting for hours for our response to their message, which I retrieved in person and transmitted to Police Higher

Command asking for the Japanese Ambassador. Always suspicious of the delay, despite my direct assurance, they were getting impatient and excitable, and gave an ultimatum over the air to Pulau Bukom — "SUNSET TIME IS BLOWING UP TIME". This was a test in a game of nerves on both sides.

From the background knowledge of the Munich Massacre, the Bukom hijackers would, inevitably, be suspicious of police action that we would be planning an attack by storming the Laju or up to trickery against them. On the ground, I remained worried they would become desperate and resort to rash action, and trigger off a disaster by blowing up the Laju in our busy harbour. I reiterated my call to Police Higher Command for response. The silence from Police HQ was deafening for me. On the ground, I hoped for the best in assuring the hijackers but was prepared for the worst, and ordered my police boats cordoning the Laju to keep a distance as we were not aware of the amount of explosives they had with them. The situation was getting increasingly precarious, as I watched the sky darkening with the setting of the sun. As the minutes passed, and evening turned to night, it was a tremendous relief for me and my men that the hijackers did not blow up the ship as they had threatened! We had stalled the hijackers by assuring and delaying tactics in my keeping up a dialogue with them. In engaging in dialogue during such a tense situation, I was mindful always to give them a 'ray of hope'.

Escalation to Higher Command

At long last, at about 10.00 pm the Japanese Ambassador finally appeared, together with Mr S R Nathan, then

Director of Security and Intelligence (MINDEF). I realised then, as I had anticipated, the case had escalated from Police HQ to Higher Command. I learnt from Mr Nathan later that it was then Permanent Secretary Home Affairs, the late Mr Tay Seow Huah, who had called him urgently while he was chairing a Board Meeting of the Mitsubishi Singapore Heavy Industries to proceed immediately to Marine Police HQ to take charge of the crisis which was unfolding. As for Mr Tay Seow Huah, he was on his way to brief the Prime Minister at the Istana. I soon became aware that I was to report directly to Mr S R Nathan who had been assigned to Marine Police HQ while Mr Tay Seow Huah, working closely as a team with him, would shuttle between the then Prime Minister Mr Lee Kuan Yew's office at the Istana, Japanese Embassy, and Marine Police HQ throughout the crisis.

Mr S R Nathan, upon his assumption of his responsibility in Marine Police HQ, decided to go with the Japanese Ambassador to the Laju to appraise and get a better feel of the situation. Unknown to the Japanese Ambassador and myself, Mr Nathan was well versed in the Japanese language. Thus, upon the approach of the Japanese Ambassador and Mr S R Nathan to the Laju, the Japanese hijackers began a long tirade about the Palestinian cause, and demanded a Japanese plane to take them out of Singapore. The Japanese Ambassador responded that he would have to contact Tokyo as this would require approval from the highest authority. The encounter ended badly with the Japanese hijackers shouting at the Japanese Ambassador and telling him to get lost. This started a series of negotiations for eight harrowing days.

From the early stage of the siege, the Japanese Government decided to opt out of the crisis, and the full burden fell squarely upon the shoulders of the Singapore Government. The impasse carried on with high tension on both sides. Neither side appeared to waver and stood firm in their position. The hijackers openly declared that they had lost all faith and confidence in the Japanese Government. The faith of the hijackers continued to vest in the Singapore Government, while we assured and undertook to help and make approaches to countries friendly to the Palestinian cause, especially the Arab nations, to resolve the crisis. It was a deep impasse and a highly intractable situation, as no country was prepared to provide safe passage for the hijackers and a plane as long as the hijackers refused to give up their arms and explosives. The track record of the PFLP in the attack on the Olympic village in Munich and the blowing up of aircraft by Palestinian terrorists was a deterrence in resolving the crisis. The intractable situation continued to persist with no solution in sight.

Attack on Japan Embassy in Kuwait

On the eve of the eighth and last day, a dramatic turn of events in favour of the hijackers took place. As no word had been heard by the Palestinian High Command from the PFLP and Japanese Red Army regarding their attack on Pulau Bukom Oil Refinery and suspecting that they had been captured, the Palestinian High Command ordered an attack on the Japanese Embassy in Kuwait. The Palestinian terrorists seized the Ambassador and the First Secretary at gun point, and threatened that unless

Japan sent a plane to Singapore immediately to free their comrades, the hijackers who had attacked the Singapore oil refinery, they would kill the Japanese hostages starting with the First Secretary.

This galvanised the Japanese into immediate action and they approached Singapore with an offer to accede to the demand of the Bukom hijackers for a plane and safe passage. This dramatic turn of events was not known to the Bukom hijackers and we ensured that we kept the news from them by withholding newspapers when it was requested by them. Had they come to know about the siege of the Japanese Embassy in Kuwait, they would have dug in their heels and hardened their stand. The Singapore Government therefore had to act swiftly. Mr S R Nathan then directed me to negotiate with the Bukom hijackers, as then Prime Minister Mr Lee Kuan Yew had decided that since no one had been killed or injured, we could agree to give them safe passage out of Singapore on condition they released all hostages and gave up all their arms and explosives.

I then met up with the Laju hijackers and told them clearly that a plane would be made available to them and that we would ensure their safe passage to Kuwait, on condition that they released all hostages and gave up all their explosives and arms. I firmly told them that if they did not accept our offer, we would wash our hands of this matter and let the Japanese take over and we would have nothing further to do with them. At first, the hijackers rejected our offer, hesitated and later asked for time to consider. I stood firm. The hijackers continued to waver, but finally agreed to accept our offer upon an agreement written and signed by me to grant them safe passage to Kuwait. Following their acceptance, discussion then focused on the hostages, and planning the route and transportation from the Laju to Marine Police HQ and then by police vehicle to the VIP lounge in Paya Lebar Airport. While the hijackers were agreeable to surrender all their explosives to us on the Laju, they were silent on the surrender of their firearms. The hijackers were under the impression that they would give up their side arms upon boarding of the plane. Mr Tay Seow Huah told me that the hijackers should be made to give up their firearms upon arrival at the Airport VIP lounge which had been specifically cleared for the purpose. The giving up of their side arms as their only safety and sole protection was highly sensitive, and we should be prepared for a shootout if the hijackers refused.

I was entrusted with the delicate task of disarming the hijackers at the VIP lounge. Fortunately, the operation went off smoothly. As I entered the VIP lounge with the hijackers, after they had released their hostages, I calmly told the Palestinian leader to give up their arms to me as no plane would take them on board if they were armed. The hijackers were clearly surprised. There was a flash of suspicion, a mixture of fear or anger in their eyes. For a moment, they thought I was out to trick them. I then grasped the arm of the Palestinian leader and reassured him that everything was alright. I repeated that if he did not trust me he could hold his Browning automatic against my temple, as a show of good faith on my part. As I grasped the Palestinian leader's hand holding the gun and in the process of directing it to my temple, he became emotional, muttered in Arabic and then said in

English: "Brother, I trust you and will give up all our arms to you." I accepted his gun with a sigh of relief. The agony was over.

Mr Nathan, who was watching the scene closely from a window in an adjoining room, then came out and told me to bring in the hijackers, one by one, and strip them of all other concealed weapons, which I did as they had knives tied to their ankles. That same night, as part of Singapore's guarantee of safe passage for the hijackers to Kuwait, 12 officials including myself under the leadership of Mr S R Nathan, took off from Paya Lebar Airport.

On Flight to Kuwait

The journey on board the JAL plane was quite uneventful as the hijackers were exhausted and kept very much to themselves. However, Mr Nathan directed me to engage in conversation with the hijackers, but he did not tell me his intention and objective at that time.

While I was talking to the hijackers, Mr Nathan joined in by cracking a joke to break the ice. I soon realised that Mr Nathan was always thinking ahead and anticipating the situation we would be confronted with upon our landing in Kuwait. Mr Nathan wanted to develop confidence with the hijackers, knowing he might need their intervention in Kuwait should we have any problems with the Kuwait authorities or the hostage takers at the Japanese Embassy in Kuwait. Mr Nathan told them that I had treated them very fairly and well, and Singapore had honoured her undertaking to guarantee and ensure their safe passage to Kuwait. They should therefore let their comrades in

Kuwait know, should we encounter problems with them upon our landing. The Bukom hijackers assured us that it would be their duty to ensure everything would be alright for us with their comrades-in-arms in Kuwait.

While nearing Kuwait, Mr Nathan was alerted to the first sign of trouble and difficulties that we would be encountering upon our arrival in Kuwait. The Japanese officials' leader, the Director-General of Gaimusho who was with us on the flight, informed Mr Nathan that he had received a message from Tokyo to the effect that the Kuwaiti Government had refused permission for anyone to disembark from our plane upon landing. On arrival, the Kuwaiti Government would put on board the Palestinian hostage takers of the Japanese Embassy in Kuwait, for the plane to fly to whatever destination they wanted. This would put us in a spot! Very soon just before landing, the Chief Pilot told Mr Nathan in despair that the air control tower in Kuwait would not allow our plane to land, and had asked the Chief Pilot to proceed to another airport. The Chief Pilot then told Mr Nathan that the plane had very little fuel left even if he wanted to fly to any other nearby airport. That being the situation, Mr Nathan told him to tell the tower that, in view of the emergency situation with the shortage of fuel, he had no choice but to land. The tower finally reluctantly agreed to let our plane land but only to refuel. As our plane was descending, I could see a huge cordon of tanks, armoured vehicles, and armed soldiers surrounding the airport in anticipation of our approach. When our plane landed, the armed cordon began to narrow and encircle our aircraft. It was like a war zone. The signal was clear. The show of force was to deter us from disembarking and/or to counteract any resistance.

Standoff Situation and Negotiation upon Landing

Upon landing, it was a long wait and stand-off situation for hours, with an eerie silence and tension-filled atmosphere prevailing. To break the silence and the standoff situation, Mr Nathan asked our Chief Pilot to establish contact with the tower to enable him to speak to someone in authority. Very soon, a voice from the tower answered and wanted to know what Mr Nathan wanted. Mr Nathan then responded saying he was the Special Envoy of the Prime Minister of Singapore and had a message for the Prime Minister of Kuwait. Tower then asked him what the message was and asked him to repeat his message to him over the air, which Mr Nathan repeatedly refused. Mr Nathan insisted that he would only convey the message to the Prime Minister in person only when he arrived at the tarmac. The man in the tower sounded angry and rebuked Mr Nathan for making things difficult for him. However, he finally relented and told Mr Nathan to wait while he conveyed his message to Higher Authority. After waiting for some time and getting no response from the tower, Mr Nathan repeated his call to the tower. After another long wait, a group of cars with flashing lights and screaming sirens, escorted a posh Cadillac with headlights on to the tarmac before our plane. It turned out that the Higher Authority was the Defence Minister and a member of the Kuwaiti Royalty. Soon after the arrival of the Defence Minister, he was joined by the Japanese Ambassador from Iran who had been designated as the envoy to deal with the crisis as the Japanese Ambassador in Kuwait had been taken hostage.

I will not go into the details and intricacies of the negotiation which started on the tarmac between the

Kuwaiti Defence Minister, the Japanese Ambassador from Iran and Mr Nathan, as I was not privy to the discussion. I knew later from Mr Nathan that it was difficult and protracted. Mr Nathan persisted in pressing his case that as Special Envoy in delivering the four Bukom hijackers to Kuwait to resolve the siege of the Japanese Embassy in Kuwait, the Kuwaiti Government had a reciprocal responsibility to ensure the safety of the Singaporean officials and therefore, whatever happened to the Singapore officials would be the responsibility of the Kuwaiti Government. The Defence Minister was annoyed and visibly angry, and threatened to arrest Mr Nathan! Mr Nathan felt strongly that his primary objective was the safety of the Singaporean officials and to get them out of the plane at all cost, instead of being forced to fly out of Kuwait Airport together with the Bukom hijackers and the Palestinian terrorists who had seized the Japanese Embassy in Kuwait. Mr Nathan was determined and continued to press home that the Singapore officials, with instruction from our Prime Minister, had come with the four Bukom hijackers who had been released and enabled to come to Kuwait to help end the siege and hostage taking at the Japanese Embassy in Kuwait. Having fulfilled our mission, all Singapore officials should be allowed to disembark and return to Singapore.

While the negotiation and protracted discussion was still going on with no end or solution in sight, the Kuwaiti Foreign Minister and his entourage arrived. Mr Nathan continued to press our case with the Kuwaiti Minister. Fortunately, this struck a positive note with the Foreign Minister, and an unexpected turn of events occurred when the Kuwaiti Minister told Mr Nathan, to go back to our plane and await his instructions. After another long wait, the Kuwaiti Foreign Minister came on board our airplane, and on seeing Mr Nathan, said: "All of you get down and get lost." Mr Nathan's agony and concern must have dissipated. We were finally allowed to leave the plane and arrangements were made for us to be picked up from our hotel later in the evening to be taken to the Kuwaiti Airport and then transferred to Bahrain Airport, where a SIA plane would transport us home. In gist, Mr Nathan as the leader of the Singapore officials through his ingenuity, diplomatic, and negotiation skill at the tarmac had performed outstandingly in finally bringing a successful end to this entire episode.

Mr S R Nathan, in his book *50 Stories from My Life*, recalled the negotiations with the Kuwaiti authorities as follows:

> When we landed, the aircraft was surrounded by tanks, armoured vehicles and soldiers carrying automatic weapons. For hours, we negotiated with the Kuwaiti authorities. I was asked to disembark from the plane and take my message in person to a Kuwaiti government minister, who was driven onto the tarmac in his limousine. Long arguments followed, involving the Kuwaitis and the Japanese Ambassador to Iran who had been brought to the scene to represent the Japanese government. The terrorists who had stormed the Japanese embassy in Kuwait arrived at the airport — and boarded the aircraft fully armed with revolvers and hand grenades. Talking to the Japanese diplomat in Bahasa, which he understood, I persuaded him to insist that they be disarmed before the

plane proceeded to its next destination. It was settled that they would keep their side arms but without the bullets — these would be kept in the hold... At last came the development we had all been waiting for. The Kuwaiti foreign minister arrived, and told me and my fellow Singaporeans to leave the aircraft. For several hours, we were afraid that the hijackers might insist that we be returned to the aircraft as hostages, so we made ourselves scarce... That night we were flown safely by Kuwait Airways to Bahrain and returned home from there on Singapore Airlines. Both groups of terrorists were flown on later to South Yemen. The whole episode ended without bloodshed. It was a good experience for me, the various ministries involved, the security service, the police, and the military. While the decision to give the Laju hijackers safe passage out of Singapore attracted some criticism, we believed it was right. We wanted to minimise any likelihood of a terrorist group picking a quarrel with Singapore and seeking retaliation (Nathan 2013, 140–141).

Mr S R Nathan as a Crisis Management Leader

Excellent leaders who are capable of handling a violent crisis, especially in dealing with professional and well-organised terrorists are rare. This is obvious, as such international situations do not happen every day. The ultimate test of a good crisis leader is only when violence erupts and the 'guns start firing', and how he responds and reacts. Does he rise to the occasion? From my interaction and having worked closely with Mr Nathan, he is, to my mind, an example of an effective crisis management leader. Mr S R Nathan, as I learnt later, was assigned by the Prime Minister's Office, as conveyed by then Permanent Secretary of Home Affairs, the late Tay Seow Huah to him, to take charge of the Laju Hijack at Marine Police Headquarters. Despite my youth and his senior status, he put me very much at ease when working throughout the crisis. Mr Nathan was calm, cool, and clear-headed throughout the crisis, and was always anticipating and thinking ahead. Mr Nathan clearly understood the dynamic nature of the crisis as it unfolded. He also clearly understood the demands and pressure confronting me as the Commander on the ground and was highly supportive of my views and recommendations in working and implementing the plans. He was a firm practitioner of empowerment on the ground, and especially where there were no precedents or guidelines. This worked out nicely for me. I believe firmly that the Commander at the frontline must be empowered to appraise, seize initiative, and make quick decisions, instead of raising everything upwards. In the nature of such crisis, the situation will always be dynamic and time is of the essence. As the ground Commander facing the crisis directly, the last thing that I would wish for is a leader who attempts to micromanage my every move. As the Commander, I faced tremendous pressure confronting the crisis, assessing the situation, and thinking on my feet as the situation developed. It would have been difficult to operate effectively if the leader I reported to directly micromanaged my every move! Fortunately, for me, Mr Nathan was an enlightened crisis leader who did not micromanage and gave me a lot of leeway to take initiative and exercise judgement in dealing with the hijackers on the ground. My personal view is that if you have no confidence in that Commander, then change him rather than micromanage his every action and tell him what to do.

In conclusion, I am of the view that Mr S R Nathan, apart from being an effective crisis leader, is a very pragmatic, humble, and down-to-earth caring man, with a deep sense of duty to our nation. He was always affable, friendly, and open, but beneath that veneer, I have no doubt, is a no-nonsense, tough, and decisive personality.

Mr Tee Tua Ba *is Chairman, Singapore Red Cross. He was a former Commissioner of Police. Mr Tee and Mr S R Nathan were part of the team that negotiated with the hijackers in the 1974 Laju Incident.*

Reflections: Social Service and Community Building

S R Nathan and His Social Service Legacy
Jennie Chua

Lessons I Learnt from Five Decades of Interaction with the Late Mr S R Nathan
K Kesavapany

A People's President Who Inspired Singaporeans to Build a Better World
Jean Tan

former Chairman of the Hindu Endowment Board and the Hindu Advisory Board. He also played a key role in the establishment of the Singapore Indian Development Association (SINDA), which has become the umbrella body looking after the educational social needs of the Indian community. I am privileged to be following in Mr Nathan's footsteps and to serve in all three institutions.

The Inter-Religious Organisation (IRO) was a body which was close to Mr Nathan's heart. As Patron of the IRO, he took a keen interest in the activities of the Organisation. Noting the rise of religious extremism and growing intolerance among faiths, Mr Nathan urged the IRO to reiterate the message of peace and harmony. With his endorsement, I was appointed a member of the IRO in 2015, one of the three representatives of the Hindu Advisory/Endowment Boards.

Advancing and Protecting Singapore's Interests through Diplomacy

In August 1972, I moved to the Ministry of Foreign Affairs, which was then located in City Hall. From this position, I was able to observe Mr Nathan in action in many situations.

The re-organisation of the Ministry of Foreign Affairs

Due to several postings abroad, Indonesia from 1973 to 1976; the Soviet Union from 1979 to 1982; the UK from 1982 to 1986, the UN (Geneva) from 1991 to 1996, I did not have many opportunities to interact with Mr Nathan in the Ministry.

I was however in HQ when he returned to MFA as Permanent Secretary, with Mr Chia Cheong Fook as Second Permanent Secretary. This was to be a momentous turning point in the life of the Ministry.

As Mr Nathan puts it in his book *An Unexpected Journey*:

> My brief was to focus on the internal workings of the organisation and shake it up to improve the quality of the work being done (Nathan 2011, 325–326).

One of the immediate measures that was instituted was the 'Morning Prayers'. This was the platform for both senior and junior officers to prove their mettle or reveal their lack of it. Everyone was kept on tenterhooks when it came to making presentations at the 'prayers'. Poor presentations earned the rebuke: "Cut out the 'palaver' and come straight to the point."

Speaking appreciatively of the young MFA diplomats under his charge, Mr Nathan added: "Whatever the issue, the people at MFA learnt their trade the hard way, in the trenches. There were few books, authorities or precedents to rely on. It was our wits that helped us move forward."

The earliest of the challenges MFA faced was the Cambodia problem following the Vietnamese invasion and occupation of that country.

Although not directly involved in the Cambodian issue, the art and craft of international diplomacy, which I witnessed, were to come in useful for me when I became Ambassador to the UN/GATT (1991–1996), and the inaugural Chairman of the General Council of the World Trade Organisation.

Be that as it may, (another favourite phrase of Mr Nathan), his second posting to MFA (1979–1982) helped to improve the profile and structure of the Ministry of Foreign Affairs. Naturally, this turn of events had a positive impact on the staff of MFA, including myself. The main lessons I learnt were the need for focus in diplomatic analysis and firmness in dealing with situations.

I must add, however, that in the non-official social interactions, Mr Nathan was all 'sugar and spice'. His attachment to family and friends is legendary. The annual Deepavali dinner that he and Mrs Nathan hosted was a high point in the social calendar.

Subsequently, as Ambassadors, Mr Nathan and I found ourselves in the frontline dealing with the Michael Fay incident — he as Ambassador to the United States, and I as Singapore's Ambassador to WTO. As Mr Nathan's role in this saga has been well documented, I will only describe the Geneva end of the story.

Upon hearing of the sentence imposed by our courts on Michael Fay, the then United States Trade Representative (USTR) Mickey Kantor exploded, and declared that Singapore would not be allowed to host the first Ministerial Conference of the WTO that had been scheduled for December 1995. Despite pleas by his own Ambassador, Booth Gardner, Kantor stood firm, and apparently remarked that the conference would be held "over my [his] dead body".

Just as Mr Nathan undertook a massive campaign to explain to the US public what the issue was all about, I lobbied every one of the 160 WTO members not to allow the USTR to hold the WTO hostage to non-trade related issues, and one involving only the United States and Singapore. When the time came for the decision to be made, all the members voted in favour of Singapore, except Ambassador Gardner who looked the other way. (This was partly because he was convinced of Singapore's justifiable case and also because we were close friends).

The moral of the story is, where a national interest is concerned, one does not buckle. Mr Nathan did not. Neither did I.

Promoting Singapore

During Mr Nathan's two terms as President, I had the privilege of hosting him and Mrs Nathan on two occasions. The first was when I was Singapore's Non-Resident Ambassador to the Hashemite Kingdom of Jordan. In November 2006, President and Mrs Nathan paid a State Visit to the Kingdom, and were warmly welcomed by His Majesty King Abdullah II and Her Majesty Queen Rania.

Upon hearing that the visit to Petra, a World Heritage site, was to be undertaken by car, the King offered two helicopters from the Royal Jordanian Air Force for the journey. At least two members of the delegation baulked at the thought of making the journey by helicopter.

Mr Nathan stood firm and said that an offer by the Royal Host should not be refused. It was a proud moment for my wife Padmini and I to have escorted our President and Mrs Nathan on this historic visit, which enhanced bilateral relations.

The second occasion when I was able to play host to Mr Nathan was in 2003 when he, as Chancellor of the National University of Singapore, led the NUS golf team to play the University of Malaya team, headed by its then Chancellor, Sultan Azlan Shah. This was during a period of tension in bilateral relations when all sporting and other exchanges were curtailed by the Malaysian side, to express the Mahathir Government's displeasure towards Singapore over a range of unresolved issues. Both the Chancellors agreed that this long-standing bilateral sporting exchange should not fall victim to political contretemps.

Although a non-golfer, Mr Nathan sportingly rode in the golf-buggy and participated in the after-golf dinner celebration. Thanks to this gracious gesture by the two Heads of State in their capacities as Chancellors, this sporting link between the two universities has grown from strength to strength.

The Institute of Southeast Asian Studies (ISEAS)

Upon returning from my six-year assignment in Malaysia, I was informed that I would be asked to take up the post of the Director of ISEAS. Apparently, President Nathan and Permanent Secretary Chia Cheong Fook (who was also Chairman of ISEAS) had felt that I would be suitable for the post.

Personally, I had some reservations as this would be the first time that a non-academic would fill this position in the Institute. I also wondered how the academic staff would react to my appointment. One staff member, in fact, felt that it would be the beginning of the politicisation of the Institute. Both President Nathan and Mr Chia Cheong Fook said that I should have no qualms about accepting the post. Throughout the 10 years of my stay in ISEAS, they gave me their full support and guidance. President Nathan also visited ISEAS whenever he could. One reason for his visit was the excellent *ikan asam pedas* cooked by ISEAS bookshop assistant, Jun, that was served during lunch!

In a handwritten note, on the occasion of my departure from ISEAS in February 2012, Mr Nathan wrote, *inter alia*, as follows:

> When I approached you in 2002 to take the leadership of ISEAS, ISEAS was in shambles, with its reputation among scholars at its lowest — no longer what it had been since its founding in 1966.
>
> In the past 10 years, you have restored ISEAS' reputation beyond expectations, such that it has the brand name of being the premier research centre on Southeast Asia, not only in this region, but beyond. Many a scholar is proud to be associated with it and its work.

After stepping down from the Presidency, Mr Nathan graciously accepted the Board's offer to be a Distinguished Fellow of the Institute and had his first office there, after leaving the Istana.

The Final Journey

After finishing his two-term Presidency, Mr Nathan returned to his original passion in public life — social service. He took a special interest in the issue of the growing income inequality that was becoming evident in the socioeconomic landscape of the country. Mr Nathan feared that, left unaddressed, this issue would have an adverse impact on the carefully cultivated social fabric of the country. Another of Mr Nathan's concerns was the position of the underclass, especially those living in one-room HDB flats. He wanted a research study to be undertaken on this issue. Whenever I visited him in hospital, it was apparent that these two concerns were uppermost in his mind. Earlier, he had commissioned a working Group (chaired by Ambassador B Jayachandran) to look into the social problems affecting the Indian community. I was a member of that Working Group.

Reflective of his concerns, Mr Nathan supported the Singapore Indian Association's 'Helping People from Falling through the Cracks' programme. Mr Nathan was to be the Guest-of-Honour for a fundraising lunch on July 9, 2015. That was not to be because shortly before that he was taken ill and hospitalised. With his demise, a pillar of support was lost, for the country, community and for myself.

Mr Nathan's legacy in the field of social work can best be encapsulated by the message he gave to Mr K V Veloo, a fellow social worker and a long-time friend:

> He made me realise that as social workers, we were little persons serving a great cause — touching lives, healing

rifts, and filling needs. It is a simple principle that has guided my journey as a social worker until today.

Like Mr Veloo, this is the greatest lesson I learnt from a man who rose from humble beginnings to become the 'People's President' of Singapore.

Mr K Kesavapany *is an Adjunct Professor at the Lee Kuan Yew School of Public Policy. Mr Kesavapany was previously Director, Insitute of Southeast Asian Studies, and worked with Mr S R Nathan at the Ministry of Foreign Affairs, during which he served in several Ambassadorial positions.*

A People's President Who Inspired Singaporeans to Build a Better World

Jean Tan

A man who kept the good of the common people close to his heart. That was how the late President of Singapore Mr S R Nathan was fondly remembered by many, and especially so at the Singapore International Foundation (SIF).

As our Patron from January 2001 to August 2011, he guided and championed our work to create greater understanding between Singaporeans and world communities to uplift lives. He truly believed in SIF's mission that we all have a part to play in building a better world — one that is peaceful, inclusive, and offers opportunities for all.

Mr Nathan was always present at SIF events, and never tired of encouraging SIF volunteers to give their all as global citizens. He was Singapore's Head of State, yet he was also down-to-earth and at ease with people — mingling, chatting, and gamely posing for photos at the SIF's events. He always made it a point to engage them with grace and warmth, telling them how important their contribution was, which certainly won their hearts.

At the 10th anniversary of one of the SIF signature programmes — Singapore International Volunteers, he said:

> Singapore's future is intertwined with that of our entire region and indeed the whole world. We are firmly committed to live in mutual support and friendship with our neighbours. We need to always ensure that we are not seen by others as fair weather friends, uncaring and unwilling to do our bit, within the limits of our ability. It is in this respect that our volunteers overseas make an invaluable contribution by way of their deeds. By coming forward to share your skills with communities overseas, you all are also ambassadors of Singapore. You show the world our human face and make the software side of Singapore better known to the world. These people-to-people relationships that you help to build are invaluable for all of us. Through you and your deeds, you have helped enhance the positive international image, and standing, of Singapore.

Since 1991, over 4,000 SIF Citizen Ambassadors that include social entrepreneurs, healthcare professionals, artists, educators, social workers and ordinary Singaporeans from all walks of life, together with friends of Singapore have worked alongside overseas communities to enable sustainable development in 17 countries. These include Afghanistan, Cambodia, China, India, Indonesia, Malaysia, Myanmar, the United States, the United Kingdom and Vietnam, in areas such as healthcare, education, arts and culture, the environment, and business and livelihood.

Many individuals within the SIF network, ranging from donors such as Deutsche Bank Asia Foundation and Singapore Airlines, programme partners like Singapore Health Services Pte Ltd (SingHeath), KK Women's and Children's Hospital, to volunteers and alumni, have been deeply touched and inspired by Mr Nathan's sincerity and passion during his 11-year patronage at the SIF.

Ms Annie Yeo, Head of Corporate Social Responsibility, Deutsche Bank Asia Foundation recounted:

> Mr Nathan's genuine interest in people and his ability at putting people around him at ease is very impressionable. I remember once at an SIF event which I attended with my younger colleagues, they were excited upon seeing the President and asked for a photo with him. Without hesitation Mr Nathan agreed but joked that he would have to charge. That sent everyone into laughter. His love for the people is clearly evident and he will forever be the People's President.

Mr Goh Choon Phong, CEO, Singapore Airlines said:

> I met Mr Nathan on a number of occasions at official events and always went away from our conversations feeling uplifted. Mr Nathan was a kind and caring man who was clearly interested in getting to know a person, no matter who that person was. Even in my brief encounters with him, I was able to get a feel for who he genuinely was — someone who cared for others, and someone who always put his service to the nation and to worthwhile causes above all else.

Adjunct Associate Professor Lim Swee Hia, Group Director of Nursing at Singhealth, said:

> A man with no airs, his ease of mixing around with volunteers and nurses is legendary. His natural warmth touched the lives of many nurses and volunteers who had the pleasure to meet and speak with him during the many events that he always graciously attends. He always has a special place in his heart for those who are less fortunate than himself.

Associate Professor Anette Jacobsen, a specialist volunteer and Chairman of the Division of Surgery, KK Women's and Children's Hospital shared:

> President Nathan is the beacon and shining light that augments our personal drive to help others in our work with SIF. Throughout his presidency, he has never lost sight of the less fortunate nor the connection with the common man. I will especially remember his quick question, which is ever forthcoming — "Do you want to take a picture with me?"

Ms Fauziah Ahmad, Principal of Rainbow Centre–Margaret Drive School added:

> At one of SIF's Appreciation Dinners, when Mr Nathan knew that I was the Principal of Rainbow Centre Yishun Park School, he actually asked me 'My wife just visited the school recently, right?' For the President of a country to remember the schools that his wife visited as part of her personal visits to special schools, he just 'wowed' me over. That's the personal touch that no other president would have except President Nathan. He's really the People's President.

Dr Celia Tan, Director at the Singapore General Hospital–Postgraduate Allied Health Institute recounted:

> It is our privilege to have him as our Patron in SIF because he inspires us to build bridges with our neighbours, especially in our work to improve their lives. He is very supportive of us as volunteers and I'm grateful for his help. I had the privilege to meet him on a few occasions and found him to be a very humble and approachable man without any airs. He has certainly left an indelible impression on the hearts of many Singaporeans.

Dr Khoo Kim Choo, a specialist volunteer and preschool Director said:

> I must have attended the annual SIF function about six times when President Nathan would preside. On every occasion, he showed genuine interest in our Early Childhood project in Myanmar and would ask thoughtful questions. He would make it a point to go around to speak to the volunteers, and I know all the volunteers present appreciated that very much.

Ms Angilay Davy d/o V Doraisamy, a specialist volunteer at a Leadership Training workshop in Indonesia, and a Senior Lecturer at the National Community Leadership Institute, recalled:

> When I went on stage to receive the certificate of appreciation as a volunteer at our volunteer night, he made an effort to connect personally with each of us. He talked to me briefly on my volunteering, and when I mentioned Indonesia, he asked me if I spoke the language and spoke to me in Bahasa. It touched me, for he stood there speaking to each of us instead of just congratulating with a handshake. To me, the President was exemplary in showing true appreciation of volunteer work.

Ms Chin Hooi Yen, Director at Gateway Law Corporation, who mentored the SIF's UNITAR Hiroshima Fellowship for Afghanistan in 2007 and 2008 said:

> At SIF events, Mr Nathan never fails to ask each of us individually questions of the work we do, takes the time to pose for one more photo, shake one more hand or give yet more words of support. He displays the spirit of dedication and selflessness that is the best of volunteerism. His sincerity is heart-warming.

Ms Nita Kapoor, SIF's programme alumni and Director General, FK Norway and Chair of FORUM, a global body of volunteer-driven development agencies who was in Singapore when SIF hosted the 2010 International Volunteer Cooperation Organisations (IVCO) said:

> I had the pleasure of meeting the President and experiencing his keen interest in the global family of IVCOs and in our work internationally. It is rare to see a patron who is so genuinely committed, engaged, and dedicated. I found it particularly inspiring to witness a person of influence using his position to encourage and inspire young volunteers in their role as global change agents.

Mr Nathan's ability to connect with people while he was President was a rare gift that, in turn, spurred our volunteers on to continue sharing their time, talents and treasures to effect real change in global communities. The SIF remains deeply honoured and grateful to Mr Nathan for his support as our Patron and as a true champion of our mission. His legacy will live on through the SIF's belief in the magic of connections to enrich lives and effect positive change.

Ms Jean Tan *is Executive Director at the Singapore International Foundation (SIF). Mr S R Nathan was Patron of the SIF.*

Reflections:
Labour and Trade Unions

Union Befriender, Media Rescuer
Peter H L Lim

Stabilising Industrial Relations
Tan Ming Hui and Stephanie Neubronner

Union Befriender, Media Rescuer

Peter H L Lim

We are in the 1960s. Singapore is moving towards independence and a merger with three territories to create the new nation of Malaysia. It is the time of Operation Cold Store. I am not a lead persona in that real-life political drama, I'm just a bit player. But I get to meet S R Nathan in a sequel to that highly-charged event.

Dawn had not broken on February 2, 1963, but the silence of the quietest part of the night had. Numerous cars and other motor vehicles started up and moved out in mini convoys to different parts of Singapore. Operation Cold Store had been unleashed. Teams of police officers, many in plainclothes, rounded up politicians and trade unionists regarded as communist or pro-communist. A few escaped the dragnet, apparently. However, 113 did not. The arrests were ordered by the Internal Security Council set up by Britain, Malaya, and Singapore. The objective: neutralise those who wanted to stop the formation of Malaysia.

Among those detained were officials of the Singapore National Union of Journalists (SNUJ), the secretary-general included. They were the more experienced ones in the union leadership. I was the SNUJ's chairman, but I was a newbie unionist. Not being on the arrest list did not spare me and other SNUJ officials from shock and anxiety. The aftershocks intensified as our branches in the Chinese-language newspapers resigned *en bloc*. Only the branch at Times House remained. Its members were the editorial staff in The Straits Times Press of newspapers and magazines. In terms of membership strength and subscription revenue, the union was considerably weakened. In terms of collective bargaining and grievance handling capabilities, the union leadership was practically disarmed. We were befuddled, too. The professionals in the company's Personnel Department had superior industrial relations firepower. They did not shy away from taking advantage of the union's sudden incapacity.

With hindsight, we could say that management missed an opportunity to extend a helping hand to the beleaguered journalists' union and thereby strengthen employer–employee relations. Also with hindsight, we concluded that management thought it safer not to be too friendly with or helpful to a union that seemed to be regarded by the authorities as anti-government. The Trades Union Movement had split. Unions were deemed to be either pro-People's Action Party or pro-Barisan Sosialis, with the vast majority in the latter group, and a few striving to remain unaligned. SNUJ, its political leanings seemingly settled by the Cold Store arrests, became a pariah in certain minds. Yet the journalists' union wanted to stay out of both camps.

About a year after Cold Store, the union leadership came reluctantly to the realisation that we urgently needed help in conducting negotiations for a new collective agreement and in handling disputes arising from members' grievances. The Labour Research Unit (LRU) was the only place to go for such guidance and assistance. The unit was set up by the Government to help all trade unions. It was not regarded by many as non-aligned, even though it was not yet part of the nascent National Trades Union Congress. In SNUJ, it was really tough getting the go-ahead from members. Freshly scarred by internal and external events, they were scared of political alignment. The leaders' lobbying among members for permission to seek LRU assistance was intense to the point of near desperation. We got the go-ahead.

Ironically, that decision by the journalists spread fearfulness over to the government side too. There were people in LRU — and way beyond that little outfit — who were highly suspicious of SNUJ's intentions in seeking assistance. Inside LRU, a vehemently-voiced view was to rebuff us. Deputy Director S R Nathan listened to his people and did his own calculations. He was seconded from the civil service. A miscalculation could damage his career prospects if SNUJ turned out to be a Trojan horse. Fortunately for the journalists, he did not allow such reservations to blunt his commitment to LRU's mission, or to suppress an innate quality of his empathy with folks in trouble.

He marshalled the pros and cons of opening the door to us, the so-called tainted union, and — I learnt of this only much later — argued that even if the SNUJ's real purpose was infiltration on behalf of 'the other side', it was a risk that LRU had to take. It had a mission; it would have to stay vigilant and take counter measures if necessary. He persuaded the Director and most of their team. Not all, for I could sense suspicion among a few of the people we were getting help from. It was much needed help that we got, including detailed briefings about employment laws, and earnest advice to avoid the inclination of many union negotiators of that era to rely on banging tables and threatening industrial action. The way to go, which has become the norm today, was doing the tedious homework to help justify claims and to argue rationally across the table, keeping tempers in check, abjuring bullying tactics.

More than a year had passed after Cold Store. The struggle for survival and dominance between NTUC and its bitter enemy, those who were wanting to establish SATU (Singapore Association of Trade Unions) was far from over. There were knife's edge situations galore. Nathan had taken a significant risk opening LRU's door to SNUJ. He was not yet involved in intelligence work. Probably, he did not have access to security assessments. Maybe I did not qualify for a whole file to myself at Special Branch, forerunner of the Internal Security Department. Yet, there were occasions when I sensed I was under surveillance. I had even caught sight of people I suspected were tailing me. For a while, when travelling in a taxi, I had easy-going chats with the driver whose cab somehow was always there when I needed one late at night.

Mr Nathan, as I called him then, was warmly welcoming when a few union colleagues and I first visited LRU. Clearly touched by the plight of the disabled SNUJ, he gave us full access to the legal, industrial relations, and street-savvy guidance that we were seeking, and also experienced people to work with. A senior teachers' union official, on secondment to LRU, even sat through all-night negotiations with us.

Soon, SNUJ acquired the ability to present its own cases in the Industrial Arbitration Court. We also had any-time-of-day-or-night access to an older LRU legal adviser who, in helping us prepare to tackle management across the table or in correspondence in the pre-email era, gave us the benefit of much practical wisdom. The next lawyer assigned to SNUJ was younger, full of updated street-savvy and the relaxed quick-on-the-draw proclivity of a movie cowboy. One day, asked yet again for advice to deal with a problem with management, he blurted out: "… The only way to reform them is for your timid lot to go on strike." *Huh*, what? We did and won. Some years later, under a new leadership, SNUJ won another strike at Times House.

Once crippled by Cold Store, SNUJ had rearmed! Albeit, with mainly defensive weapons in its armoury. The walking wounded that Nathan tended to and gave a 'Fully recovered, much stronger now' medical certificate was just one of his many accomplishments and contributions to our trade union movement. I, the SNUJ official who benefited so much from interactions with him personally and professionally, was heartbroken when I read Chapter 8 of his 2011 book *Winning Against the Odds: The LRU in NTUC's Founding*, 'Building up a core of industrial relations officers'. He describes at the end of the chapter, in genteel words, his disenchantment with NTUC and the trigger for his return to the civil service in 1965. However, he continued to serve NTUC in various part-time and *ad hoc* situations until February 1988, when he was appointed High Commissioner to Malaysia. Recalling Nathan's own words in his book:

> Here and elsewhere in this monograph I have referred to occasions when NTUC officials stirred up trouble or abused me for doing something which Devan Nair (the Secretary-General) had instructed me to do. In none of these cases did Devan Nair take any steps against them, reprimand them or discipline them in any way… I took his behaviour in good spirit because I knew of the struggle that he was waging against the pro-Communist leftists. In that fight he might have considered certain people useful despite their thuggishness — indeed their approach was sometimes necessary in the confrontation with the other side. Perhaps that was justification enough… I would not wish to give the reader the impression that he let me down without justification… he may have considered it wiser to leave it to me to understand the wider context against which I should take what appeared to be misplaced behaviour (Nathan 2011, 119–120).

That passage reveals the indomitable spirit of S R Nathan. Though his feelings were badly bruised by the resistance to his efforts to professionalise the union movement's frontline troops, the industrial relations officers, he worked flat out to help organise the International Labour Seminar. The seminar took place just two months after Singapore's separation from Malaysia in 1965. Deficient in international contacts, funds, and experience in putting together such a big conference, and in such a hurry — but not lacking in detractors at home and abroad — NTUC pulled it off. The list of 'Very Crucial Attendees' included big personalities in the Afro-Asian world. That world then was split between the pro-Communists and the anti-communists, with a minor third force, the non-communists which included Singapore. They all called themselves non-aligned. It was crucial for the new nation of Singapore to make friends across the globe. Nathan proved time and again over the decades that he was a befriender extraordinary.

Nathan and I were total strangers when we first met at LRU. After that, our friendship deepened. I was constantly inspired by his sense of mission, his dedication to duty, his grasp of the most complex essentials, his open mind — and a unique core strength, his quiet courage in interactions with people high up or humble. Interactions in service to nation or simply in the course of day-to-day human contact. As a friend who was also a news contact, he was constantly on guard not to cross lines with me. On the newspaper side, I did not expect favours or open support that would compromise his official position. However, we were close enough friends for him to call me one day and, uncharacteristically, asked for a personal favour: would I take his young children Juthika and Osith for a drive in the company car that was equipped with a radio-telephone and let them make just one call each? That was years before today's mobile phones. The four of us — the Nathan kids, the company driver and I — had a really good time!

In early 1982, it was heartbreak time for me again. My initial reaction to the changed circumstances hurt S R Nathan deeply. I had been calling him S R for years.

Then, in the new situation, I started calling him Chairman at work, except when we were alone with each other, for Prime Minister Lee Kuan Yew had sent him to The Straits Times Press as the company's Executive Chairman. Thus he became the boss of my boss, the group's chief executive. The newly appointed Executive Chairman's roles were to act as the Government's monitor in the newsrooms and to help ensure the newspapers' continuing success.

A prequel to the Executive Chairman episode: in 1973, Singapore's three bus companies merged to form the monopolistic Singapore Bus Services. It was a shotgun wedding even though pregnancy was not the cause. The Government man seconded to organise the marriage and to ensure its consummation was one of the brightest young stars in the civil service then. He had with him other civil servants. They were referred to as the Government Team of Officials — GTO. The term outlived the bus monopoly, for the sole bus company found itself with a new rival after some years when Government decreed that a duopoly would be better for commuters.

Almost a decade later, the term 'GTO' resurfaced as Government prepared to send a team of monitors into Times House. There was no announcement, but our reporters started gathering bits and pieces of information about the preparations. As the itsy-bitsy facts sprouted tendrils, reporters and editors began to make connections. A picture formed. Still fuzzy, the scenario grew increasingly alarming. We learnt that a Permanent Secretary, one who was regarded by journalists as usually stern with media folks, was to command the GTO. To be posted to the company was a ministry's deputy secretary. She was to be appointed The Straits Times Press' joint Managing Director — a post that did not exist — and she was to have a desk adjacent to that of the managing director so she could understudy him.

Managing Director L J Holloway, Denis Tay who headed the marketing team then called the Advertisement Department, my deputy Cheong Yip Seng, and I, then the group's editor-in-chief, met after office hours for more than a few huddles. There were two main companies in the group, then known as Times Organisation. The other was Times Publishing, which encompassed subsidiaries and associates such as Times Printers. Lyn — as some of us called the MD — was also chief executive of Times Publishing. Apart from the four of us, no one else from the group was asked to join our 'how to survive' discussions.

'How to survive' is not overdramatising the crisis. What was at stake for us in 1982 was not corporate life-or-death, but the survival of the soul of the newspaper that was founded in colonial Singapore 1845. The soul of a newspaper is journalism in its ideal form: tell the readers what really happened and what it all means. That is the mission that transcends all the variations of time, ideologies, cultures, and intellectual space that make freedom of information an eternally controversial issue. The more thoughtful journalists and publishers understand that and — not all of them, though — commit themselves to the mission. The abiding faith for Singaporean journalists is that, if there is room for meaningful journalism, do not quit!

I did quit, after S R Nathan arrived at Times House. Here is an extract of his account of how it transpired, in words so serene from his 2011 book *An Unexpected Journey: Path to the Presidency*.

> It was around the end of October 1981. I was still working as First Permanent Secretary in the Ministry of Foreign Affairs. One Saturday evening, I had a phone call from Peter Lim… I was at home that night, just about to have dinner, and assumed that he was phoning me at this unusual time to clarify some news item relevant to my own work, as he did occasionally.
>
> Peter went straight to the point. He and his boss, managing director Lyn Holloway… had a meeting with the Prime Minister, Lee Kuan Yew, at the Istana that afternoon. The meeting, one of a number, was to discuss the government's unhappiness with the slanted aspects of the paper's news coverage and editorial comment, unfairly critical of the government and its policies on domestic affairs. During the meeting, Peter said, Holloway had urged Peter to tell the Prime Minister that he (Peter) had asked me to consider joining *The Straits Times* after my retirement from government. Peter said that the Prime Minister was planning to put a senior civil servant into the company's top management. He apologised to me for putting my name instead to the Prime Minister without my prior permission — he hoped I would not in any way be embarrassed. The implication of this conversation was that the Prime Minister might well be sending me to *The Straits Times*.

Peter's account of the Istana conversation came to me as a complete surprise. According to him, the Prime Minister's initial reaction had been sceptical. He had laughed, and asked, in effect, why would I or any other permanent secretary want to join *The Straits Times*? Peter had told him that we (Peter and I) had had a preliminary discussion about my joining the newsroom, after my retirement, as a mentor to journalists covering national and international affairs, and that I could also write in-depth columns and commentaries for the paper.

On the phone that Saturday night, I listened to what Peter had to report. I made no immediate comment. He said: 'You're not saying anything!' I replied that as he had so informed the Prime Minister there was nothing for me to say (Nathan 2011, 449–450).

The five Saturday afternoons that the Prime Minister devoted to the conversations with Lyn and me about his unhappiness with *The Straits Times* and Times House newsroom culture featured none of the 'beware my karate chop' thunder that had won him C V Devan Nair's fond nickname for him: Chief Thundercloud! Instead, the earnest discussions were peppered with long moments of warmth and even charm, some classy as well as somewhat crude humour, and even a lengthily detailed account of how he finally managed to get the Istana grounds' grass to grow evenly after he had moved office from City Hall to the Annexe.

On a Saturday when Lyn was excused from the meeting because he had a cold — as I was on another Saturday — the Prime Minister said that Nathan would be going to *The Straits Times*, "but as your boss, not your employee" (or words to that effect). He paused, as if waiting for a reaction from me. I had an instant reaction, it was welling in my gut, but I was frantically trying to choose my words. The pause seemed overly long. The Prime Minister looked intently into my eyes, put a raised finger to his lips, as if to say "Don't say!" I did not. We shook hands, I said "Thank you, Mr Lee", he nodded and I left his office. His security officers outside and I exchanged smiles.

Two paragraphs from S R's book *An Unexpected Journey* reveal in sharp focus Prime Minister Lee Kuan Yew's double-handed approach. One virtually with a clenched fist, the other with the open palm that offers a healing touch. The paragraphs are in Chapter 6. Nathan was told that: "He was willing to send in a government team to cut out the rot if necessary, and that he would give me a month in which to assess the situation." Nathan was also told that *The Straits Times* "has 150 years of history. It has been a good paper. It is like a bowl of china. If you break it, I can piece it together. But it will never be the same. Try not to destroy it."

I withdrew my resignation soon after Nathan came. Staying on in 1982 instead of going to the United States as a refugee from Singapore-style media controls gave me the opportunity to deepen my appreciation of S R's quiet courage. His mental and physical courage as displayed in the Laju hijack episode is well known. His opening the door to the tainted Singapore National Union of Journalists after Operation Cold Store was also courage of a high order — but of a different genre. Not the war zone or high human drama, easily recognisable kind that we all salute, but the silent courage of conviction reinforced by an abundance of empathy for fellow human beings and the daring not to just follow orders, but to do the needful rightfully.

S R himself had related the awesome metamorphosis that he had to undergo at Times House: "The transition from being a Permanent Secretary in a major government ministry, with considerable power and authority exercised within a clearly defined hierarchy, to being a somewhat unwelcome newspaper chairman tasked to perform delicate surgery on an organisation made up of intelligent, opinionated, and creative individuals, was a stark one" (Nathan 2011, 459). It was indeed. His "delicate surgery" (Nathan 2011, 459) was a six-year-long operation with multifarious dimensions. The patient survived.

He had also said that he was "not greeted with open arms" (Nathan 2011, 459) when he first arrived. That was an understatement. There were no open arms from the editorial staff. More hurtful for him was that board members and senior management, too, were generally unwelcoming. There were also hurtful situations caused by acts of commission or omission by the government side. When he left for higher callings in 1988, he was missed by many journalists who had lived through the trauma, had not forgotten the darkness, but who had reason to be grateful that he had come.

S R's legacy in the former *Straits Times* newsrooms is that of a rescuer who had come just in time, at first assigned by the PM to bring us to heel, ending up as the healer with an antidote — I am borrowing someone's elegant word — an antidote that helped to clear toxins debilitating government–press relations. And, which also revived faith that there's room for meaningful journalism.

Mr Peter Lim *is the founding Chief Editor of The New Paper and former Editor-in-Chief of The Straits Times. Mr Lim worked with Mr S R Nathan when the latter was at the Labour Research Unit, and later when they were both at The Straits Times.*

Stabilising Industrial Relations

Tan Ming Hui and Stephanie Neubronner

A Period of Political Turmoil

The years leading up to Singapore's independence marked a period of great political change, frequent strikes and unpredictability, as intense rivalry panned out between the pro-Communist left and the non-Communists.[1] The trade unions took centre stage of this bitter political strife. Capitalising on unstable industrial relations, a divided labour movement, and economic grievances of the workers, the pro-Communists politicised industrial disputes in a bid to discredit the People's Action Party (PAP) and to foster hatred towards the government. As Mr S R Nathan recalled in his book, *Winning Against the Odds: The Labour Research Unit* in NTUC's Founding:

> Even in strikes not started by the communists, left-wing influence was often at work. For example, when city

---

[1] See Daljit Singh and V T Arasu, ed., *Singapore: An Illustrated History* (Singapore: Information Division, Ministry of Culture, 1984); John Drysdale, *Singapore: The Struggle for Success* (Singapore: Marshall Cavendish International (Asia) Pte Ltd, 2010); Dennis Bloodworth, *Tiger and the Trojan Horse* (Singapore: Times Editions-Marshall Cavendish, 2005).

council workers went out on strike, pro-Communist union leaders put pressure on 14 of the city council unions to be more militant. They sent their leaders to meet council union leaders to intensify, prolong and aggravate the disputes (Nathan 2011, 30).

It was in December 1961, when Mr Nathan, then a young civil servant, was asked to join the newly-established Labour Research Unit (LRU) as its Assistant Director. The LRU was set up as an autonomous institution to serve the needs of trade unions and to prevent them from falling under communist influence. Mr Nathan was known to have sympathies for the workers and was selected for the job precisely because of that.

Maintaining a Delicate Balance

Despite the lack of clear directions on what the job entailed, Mr Nathan accepted his new responsibilities earnestly, and set out to resolve complex and wide-ranging issues faced by the unions. Initially, he found himself caught between his position as a neutral civil servant and an advocate for workers' rights. In his book *An Unexpected Journey: Path to Presidency*, he described his conflicted feelings and later, his decision to act openly for the workers:

> I recognised the role the LRU was performing, and I accepted that I too had a role to play, given the unpredictable political situation of the time and the growing agitation by pro-Communist unions bent on creating political instability. And in discharging this responsibility, I knew that the LRU was helping many working people and their families in one way or another (Nathan 2011, 238–239).

In his difficult role as a LRU official, Mr Nathan needed to minimise the loss of man hours, disruptions to the developing economy, and prevent incidents of stoppages or violence that strikes and demonstrations were causing. At the same time, he also needed to ensure that the working conditions of the workers were fair, that their rights were protected, and that resolutions to disputes were acceptable. In *An Unexpected Journey*, he recounted some of the challenges he faced in maintaining this delicate balance:

> Sometimes my trade union clients needed to be persuaded about the weakness of a demand. I had to be careful in such cases not to give any reason for them to think that I was taking this line because of some partiality towards their employers or the government (Nathan 2011, 243–244).

He rose to the occasion. Applying immense patience, tolerance, and flexibility, he worked tirelessly to develop trust and good working relationships with the unionists, many of whom had preferred making thuggish and militant threats to attain their goals. He persuaded them to seek reasonable demands through proper grievance procedures and to resolve disputes with peaceful settlements.

Gaining Workers' Support and Training Industrial Relations Officers

On many occasions, Mr Nathan was asked to enter into quiet discussions with employers and other parties. Despite these actions being viewed as "a betrayal of the trust the unions had placed on me to fight their cause to the bitter end", Mr Nathan regarded these attempts at seeking reconciliation as necessary and pertinent to preventing issues from getting out of control.

In his book *Winning Against The Odds*, Mr Nathan articulated the increasing difficulties he faced:

> My initial challenge at the LRU was how to provide a service to trade union leaders whose demands were in fact unreasonable. In time, the mission turned out to be even more complicated, from purely rendering advice and help in collective bargaining and matters before the Industrial Arbitration Court, the Unit was gradually sucked into a more proactive role in the struggle to win the support of workers in the newly established industrial enterprises across Singapore and at Jurong in particular (Nathan 2011, 65).

Mr Nathan also expressed concerns over the mismatch in language competency and skills to negotiate with unionists preventing the support of workers' interests. Recognising the need to get unions to stop using the crude confrontation tactics they were engaging in, Mr Nathan was certain that the only way negotiations could be carried out in a more civilised manner was to establish a corps of properly trained Industrial Relations Officers.

Utilising a trip he made to Europe in late 1964, Mr Nathan arranged to visit a number of unions to assess if they had training programmes that could be adapted for use in Singapore. Mr Nathan, however, found that none of the unions abroad trained their negotiators. Even so, these trips were not entirely fruitless. Mr Nathan met two professors, whom he introduced to the National Trades Union Congress's (NTUC) founding Secretary-General, Mr Devan Nair. These introductions lead to the eventual establishment of the Singapore Institute of Labour Studies, which is now known as the Ong Teng Cheong Labour Leadership Institute.

The first group of Industrial Relations Officers of the LRU were seconded from the Singapore Teachers' Union and various commercial house unions for one year at a time. Still, Mr Nathan felt that this arrangement was not sustainable as he felt that "the NTUC needed to develop its own corps of activists, potential leaders and negotiators, fully competent in various aspects of union work, including working on the ground" (Nathan 2011, 278). Moreover, these "activists were part-timers and largely English-educated", which did not satisfy the needs of the growing Chinese-educated workforce (Nathan 2011, 279).

In his book *An Unexpected Journey*, Mr Nathan further described the importance and need for suitably trained individuals. Nevertheless, he recognised that the NTUC did not have the financial resources to engage such individuals or initiate such a training programme. Mr Nathan knew that if funds were to be obtained from the government, only the LRU was able to assist the NTUC in this endeavour. Mr Nathan promptly initiated discussions with Mr Nair and presented a paper to Dr Goh Keng Swee, then Minister for Finance, outlining the plans and the kind of funding that would be needed.

When the plan was approved, Mr Nathan drew up a scheme to engage about 20 to 30 candidates who would be paid on a government scale for executive officers and were direct employees of the LRU. Specifying the need for these candidates to have Nanyang University degrees, get security clearance so as to prevent pro-Communist infiltration, and also to undergo leadership training in the National Youth Leadership Training Institute at Buona Vista, Mr Nathan oversaw the entire recruitment process. Emphasising his commitment towards understanding and meeting the needs of workers, Mr Nathan attributed his earlier work experience handling seamen's disputes as being immensely useful in his handling of such matters in the LRU.

Ms Tan Ming Hui *and* **Ms Stephanie Neubronner** *are Associate Research Fellows at the S. Rajaratnam School of International Studies. This essay is adapted from Mr S R Nathan's accounts of his stint at the LRU in his books, Winning Against the Odds (2011) and An Unexpected Journey (2011).*

Reflections: Media

Diplomat, Media Boss, and President
Yang Razali Kassim

Bridging Media and Government: S R Nathan's Unique Role
Han Fook Kwang

Diplomat, Media Boss, and President

Yang Razali Kassim

The first time I met S R Nathan was in 1980 on the steps of City Hall. I was then fresh out of university, looking for a job, possibly in the Ministry of Foreign Affairs. I do not know how, but my feet brought me to that stately building. As a young graduate, I had heard of the name 'S R Nathan' with some awe. As fate would have it, I bumped into him on the way up. He surprised me by approaching me first. Far from his fearsome reputation, he struck me as someone friendly, even warm.

I did not join the Ministry of Foreign Affairs (MFA), ending up instead with *The Straits Times* (ST). While waiting for a reply from MFA, the newspaper had offered me a position in its Foreign Desk, which I took up. I was assigned to write on regional and international affairs, apart from assessing and selecting copy from the wire agencies, 'copy tasting', for use in the foreign news pages. I was later to learn that this was to hone a rookie's skill in the art of developing news sense. It also exposed us to tight and sharp writing — something which I later learned that S R Nathan was insisting at MFA from his diplomats.

From Diplomacy to the Media World

Barely two years into my job, *The Straits Times* was abuzz with talk of problems with then Prime Minister Lee Kuan Yew. It later transpired that then Editor-in-Chief Peter Lim was resisting a possible takeover of the newspaper by the Government. On February 8, 1982, *The Straits Times* carried a front-page, single column report: "Nathan to join Straits Times Board" as Executive Chairman. That immediately evoked fear in the newsroom, as if doomsday was coming.

Apart from the tension between *The Straits Times* leadership and PM Lee, who was upset among other things with the paper's coverage of Government policies, the name S R Nathan itself generated unease on the editorial floor. No doubt he was coming from MFA where he had just stepped down as first Permanent Secretary; but Nathan's other reputation was that of the man who also came from an intelligence background prior to MFA. He was seen as someone who had come with a specific mission — to be a watchdog over *The Straits Times*. His entry into the media world was greeted with dismay by journalists. Indeed, Nathan was to later note in his autobiography *An Unexpected Journey: Path to the Presidency* that he was an "unwelcome newspaper chairman" whose coming was greeted by a protest by the journalists wearing black armbands (Nathan 2011, 459).

Actually, Nathan's entry into *The Straits Times* was a compromise of sorts between PM Lee and Chief Editor Peter Lim. The PM had told Peter that he was planning to send a government team to take it over — unless *The Straits Times* shaped up. To prevent this, Peter had proposed to PM Lee that he be allowed to bring in a mentor from the Government whom he knew very well. That person would be S R Nathan. According to Nathan in his book, PM Lee agreed but assigned Nathan to join *The Straits Times* more than just as a mentor. He was to be Executive Chairman, with "full powers to intervene" (Nathan 2011, 451).

When Nathan took up his post in *The Straits Times*, Peter submitted his resignation straightaway. "I felt a sense of personal failure, as it was part of my mission to maintain as much editorial independence as possible," Peter later told staff. He, however, retracted his resignation subsequently. It transpired that Nathan was hurt; he had told a few people that Peter should not have resigned after having wanted him to join *The Straits Times* in the first place. Painful it might have been, that kind of hurt feeling could only have been between close friends. Indeed, their friendship harked back to their days in the unions; while Peter was head of the union of journalists, Nathan was heading the labour movement at NTUC's Labour Research Unit. In other words, Nathan's entry into the media world was both an assignment as well as a favour to a friend — a tricky combination if not handled well.

From 'Watchdog' to 'Native'

To his credit, in the six years that he served as The Straits Times Press' Executive Chairman, Nathan was neither a government watchdog nor a task-master. In fact, he saw his mission as someone who would be a bridge-builder between the media and the Government. "I also wanted to dispel the idea that I favoured letting the local press turn into a mere outlet for official statements and information", Nathan says in his book (Nathan 2013, 144). In short, he would not want *The Straits Times* under him to turn into a Government mouthpiece. Nathan assured *The Straits Times* that he would not interfere in the running of the editorial floor. That assurance was crucial as it calmed down the journalists' anxiety. In fact, on a number of occasions, Nathan turned out to be a fierce defender of the newspaper when policymakers or even ministers proved unreasonable.

Nathan scrupulously kept a distance from the editorial floor. His office was at the opposite end of its entrance, in a new wing refurbished for him — near where the Foreign Desk was located. To get to his office, he would enter by the new wing's own entrance, which meant bypassing the editorial floor. Occasionally, Nathan would nevertheless walk through the editorial floor, past the Foreign Desk. When he did so, our paths would sometimes cross, and he would pause for a chat, to make small talk, and offer his views on issues of the day. For the Executive Chairman to do so with a junior journalist like me spoke a lot about him. Despite all the misgivings about his presence in ST, Nathan struck me as a friendly and caring boss, not the mean one that his reputation made him out to be.

Indeed, Nathan, ever the dutiful person, was playing a crucial role. This time, his duty was to be the man who would rebuild the frayed relationship between the press and Government. "He cleared up a lot of suspicions the Government had about how the papers were run. He turned out more to be a bridge than a watchdog", Peter said. In fact, so protective had Nathan become of the media that civil servants complained that Nathan had "switched sides". In fact, on his resignation from *The Straits Times* to be High Commissioner to Malaysia, one headline in 1988 flashed: "Press watchdog turns 'native'". "They found he wasn't much of an ogre — and that, yes, it was possible to be human and pro-Government", Peter Lim said.

From Civil Servant to President

Over the years, there were to be a few other occasions when I had the opportunity to meet him again. When S R Nathan went on to be Singapore's Ambassador to Washington, DC after serving in Kuala Lumpur, we met in Seattle when I was part of the media delegation covering Prime Minister Goh Chok Tong on his visit to the US. Nathan was then on the diplomatic forefront fighting the flak triggered by the Michael Fay affair. Upon his return to Singapore in 1996, Nathan was invited by then Defence Minister Tony Tan to help set up a new think tank, the Institute of Defence and Strategic Studies (IDSS). It was later to be known as the S. Rajaratnam School of International Studies (RSIS), named after Singapore's first Foreign Minister whom Nathan served. In RSIS, Nathan was to later become a Distinguished Senior Fellow, after he stepped down from the presidency, until his passing on August 22, 2016.

My lasting impression of S R Nathan was of him as the sixth President of Singapore. I noted a transformation in his persona. Gone was the image of a stern public servant. Enter S R Nathan, the national leader. As head of state, he took to the role like fish to water. Through his years in government and the media, the only language I had heard him speak was English, which he did eloquently. However, as president, he impressed me with his Malay — so fluent was he in the national language, though this was not surprising coming from someone of his generation. I also heard him speak in Tamil on television — something I personally had not the chance to hear him speak publicly before. Indeed, it was not off the mark to see him as the 'People's President', someone with a fatherly demeanour as he strove to be the President for all Singaporeans.

S R Nathan had a natural inclination to help the working class and the less fortunate, having had a tough upbringing as a child. As President, he made it his mission to raise funds for the disadvantaged. Thus was born the 'President's Challenge'. Corporations and philanthropists were invited to donate to a cause he would champion and the funds so raised would be distributed to organisations in need of assistance. What started off as an *ad hoc* project became so successful that it is now an annual affair. Word had it that he was also an anonymous donor, helping people in need without publicity and fanfare. In this, he reminded me of the Malay community's Islamic ethic of "helping with the right hand without the left hand knowing".

Deputy Prime Minister Tharman Shanmugaratnam described S R Nathan as "deeply multiracial". I could not agree more. In his presidential persona, he touched everyone's hearts, including the Malay/Muslim community. Indeed, not known to many except some leaders, the community was one of those he assisted a lot. I did not know that he had a deep concern for the Malay/Muslim community, until he called me one day to the Istana. He was visibly anxious about the slow support being marshalled for a community book project that he was fond of. He asked whether I could work with the book editor and see what could be done. Nathan also said that he would be backing it with funds from the President's Challenge.

The book eventually was published — an impressive collection of well-researched articles entitled *The Malay Heritage of Singapore*. Despite being Indian, he was in his own indirect way, as much a leader for the Malay community in his capacity as President of Singapore. I have no doubt that had the community needed another mentor from the pioneer generation, S R Nathan would have easily fit into that role.

Mr Yang Razali Kassim *is a Senior Fellow at the S. Rajaratnam School of International Studies. Mr Yang Razali previously worked with Mr S R Nathan at The Straits Times.*

Bridging Media and Government: S R Nathan's Unique Role

Han Fook Kwang

When Mr S R Nathan was asked in 1981 by the Prime Minister to take up a new appointment in the country's main newspaper, *The Straits Times*, the challenge must have seemed particularly daunting. He had no experience running a paper and he knew the journalists there would view him with suspicion and hostility. A government man who had previously been head of intelligence brought in to make the paper toe the government line? That was the talk in the newsroom.

A lesser man might have found a way to decline the mission. However, Mr Nathan could not say no to Mr Lee Kuan Yew. At their final meeting before he took up his appointment, the PM had these parting words for him: "Nathan, I am giving you *The Straits Times*. It has 150 years of history. It has been a good paper. It is like a bowl of china. If you break it, I can piece it together. But it will never be the same. Try not to destroy it" (Nathan 2011, 458).

What was Mr Nathan's response? This was what he wrote in his memoirs *An Unexpected Journey*:

> I said nothing. He said, 'You are keeping silent.' I said, 'Sir, you have told me what to do. Also what not to do. What is there for me to say.' And so I left (Nathan 2011, 458).

And so he left the orderly, disciplined world of the public service for the messy, free-wheeling world of journalism. However, it was journalism, Singapore style, with a Government which had very strong, often unyielding views of the role of the press in Singapore society. It did not accept the Western idea of the mass media as a watchdog of the Government, but expected it to play a constructive nation-building role. Mr Lee was unapologetic about this approach when he told a conference of international editors and journalists in Helsinki in 1971:

> Freedom of the press, freedom of the news media must be subordinated to the overriding needs of the integrity of Singapore and to the primacy of purpose of an elected government.

Mr Nathan would become Executive Chairman of The Straits Times Press in 1982, tasked to improve its relations with the Government. The PM had told him that he had two major concerns with the paper. First, that it was trying to pre-empt Government policy announcements by scooping the news through investigative journalism and presenting them in a negative light. Second, Mr Lee believed the newsroom was not up to the job, and wanted to improve the quality of local journalists and have more of them who understood the issues confronting a young country without any resources. For someone who had never been in journalism, they were tall orders. How did he go about this task? He proved to be a patient, skilful, and shrewd operator who instinctively understood the nature of the problem and how it could be solved. Mr Nathan did not go into the paper with guns blazing, removing journalists who were troublesome. Instead, he took his time to understand the newsroom culture, talking to people, especially with senior editors, building up his relationship with them and gaining their trust.

A few examples illustrate his modus operandi. A month after joining the paper, he was asked by Foreign Minister S Dhanabalan what progress had been made. The PM had wanted to know. Mr Nathan said he was still new and needed more time to understand the root of the problem. Even at this early stage, he told the Minister firmly that he did not see the need for a Government team to come in and clean up things. "I said I was against throwing out people arbitrarily and would only do so if there was real evidence of bias or mischief in their reporting", he wrote in his memoirs. Indeed, he also defended the local management team, telling Mr Dhanabalan that they were generally well-disposed to the government and understood what was in the national interest. He was sticking his neck out, but it was not out of blind faith for *The Straits Times* team, but based on what he was able to gather in that one short month. It helped that, whatever his assignments, Mr Nathan was always a hands on person, prepared to put in his shift. At *The Straits Times*, he worked six days a week — including Saturdays, even though it was a day off for senior management at the paper — arriving around 9.30 am every day and working well past 8.00 pm. This was how he put it in his memoirs:

> Complex though the situation was, it was clear to me that the solution did not lie in an administrative clean-up, arbitrary measures or dismissals. I realised that insensitive handling of the situation could have adverse repercussions beyond the company.
>
> It took time, but gradually Peter Lim (the paper's Editor-in-Chief) and his colleagues came to appreciate that I was there to work with them to address their problems and not usurp their functions. I was not there simply to impose solutions derived from my previous experience. Gradually, the atmosphere began to improve (Nathan 2011, 464–465).

It required political courage to work with the editors and be seen to be doing so during a period when the government thought so poorly of the press.

Another example of his willingness to get his hands dirty and to face the problem squarely was over a story *The Straits Times* did on how expatriate staff at the National University of Singapore felt about the university. The paper had published the story without any comments from the university management, but it was not for lack of trying. The reporter had asked but none was forthcoming, and after waiting for several days, the story was published. Mr Nathan received a phone call from a very upset vice chancellor, Professor Lim Pin, who had himself been spoken to by a furious Dr Tony Tan, the Education Minister. When the paper decided to do a second story based on an interview with Professor Lim,

Dr Tan requested to see a draft of the story prior to publication. However, that would have set a bad precedent and Peter Lim refused. Mr Nathan was forced to intervene.

> I asked Dr Tan if we would withdraw that request provided I undertook to review it myself, personally. He agreed. According to Peter, when he phoned Dr Tan to thank him for his understanding, the response was to the effect, "I do not understand at all. I'm only agreeing to this because Nathan suggested it" (Nathan 2011, 470).

As Peter Lim recounted during a forum last December, it required a different kind of courage from the one Mr Nathan displayed during the hijacking of the ferry, Laju, in which he faced physical danger. This was steadfast political courage, to stand up for principles he believed in and putting the paper's interest before his. He could have ordered Peter to allow Dr Tan to see the piece and score points with his political masters. However, he stood his ground. He also went about quietly improving the quality of the newsroom, helping to recruit promising people from the civil service and making changes to the way senior people used their sabbaticals so that they would benefit professionally. I did not know it at the time but Mr Nathan had a hand in recruiting me to *The Straits Times* in 1989. He told me this when I visited him in hospital last year about a month before he passed away. He did not elaborate but with his wide network in the public service and his close relationship with permanent secretaries of the various ministries, it was not difficult for him to obtain a list of civil servants who could be targeted for recruitment.

He helped to build bridges with the government, meeting regularly with then Deputy Prime Minister Goh Chok Tong, Information and Communication Minister Yeo Ning Hong, and other Ministers. During these meetings, he would often take the hit over government's unhappiness with the paper's reporting but, as he recounted, he "had to take the criticisms in a positive spirit".

Mr Nathan's legacy in his six years in *The Straits Times* is an important one. He helped the paper ride over a rough patch in its relation with the government, which made it unnecessary to send in its own team of civil servants to run the paper, which it had earlier planned to do. That would have been disastrous and a huge setback for the paper. He persuaded editors that it was possible to do meaningful journalism within the constraints of operating in Singapore with its strict media laws. However, doing this well requires a quality newsroom with journalists who understood national issues at a deeper level and produce thoughtful, credible pieces relevant to the readership. He helped develop this professionalism. More importantly, he demonstrated that doing credible journalism in Singapore required newspaper bosses to support and back their editors and journalists in the face of political pressure. Mr Nathan understood this well. He was not afraid to get his hands dirty and to stand up for the paper.

When he left the paper in 1988, the newsroom was sorry to see him go. The man they had feared would come in to do a hatchet job for the Government had turned out to become one of their trusted allies.

Mr Cheong Yip Seng who had succeeded Peter as Editor-in-Chief wrote this farewell note:

> You helped restore confidence among our journalists. You showed us that our values as journalists and the goals of government are not incompatible. You came as 'supremo'. The newsroom was fearful: would you be like an army general in a company staffed by largely creative, not so orderly people? Their fears were unfounded. You led, but carried us along with you. You did not rely on clout but reason.

Mr Nathan's approach to Government–press relations and the values he stood for are as relevant today as they were 30 years ago. Indeed, they might be even more important today when the political landscape is more complex and competitive and the media scene has been completely transformed as a result of the Internet and social media. The mass media now is under greater pressure to maintain its credibility and relevance. The Government too is under greater pressure from a more demanding electorate. Government-press relations will have to adjust and respond to these new challenges.

Mr Nathan would have understood this.

Mr Han Fook Kwang *is a Senior Fellow at the S. Rajaratnam School of International Studies. Mr Han is also Editor-at-Large of The Straits Times.*

Reflections:
Research and Academia

A Man For All Seasons
Kumar Ramakrishna

S R Nathan and the Institute of Defence and Strategic Studies (IDSS): The Formative Years
Ang Cheng Guan

Nurturing a New Generation of Scholars
Joseph C Y Liow, Bernard Loo, and Bhubhindar Singh

A Man For All Seasons

Kumar Ramakrishna

My first formal meeting with S R Nathan, then Director of the fledgling Institute of Defence and Strategic Studies (IDSS) was in 1998, when I was a postgraduate student on a MINDEF scholarship in London. In June that year, I had had a fortuitous meeting in Senate House, the University of London, with a historical figure: Chin Peng, the Secretary-General of the Communist Party of Malaya (CPM).

For four decades, from 1948 till 1989, the CPM had been technically at war with both Malaya (later Malaysia) and Singapore. The BBC had wanted to produce a documentary commemorating the 50th anniversary of the outbreak of the so-called Malayan Emergency and its producers had tracked Chin Peng down in Thailand with a view to interview him. As a *quid pro quo*, the then 74-year-old CPM leader had asked to visit the historical archives in London, as well as meet eminent historians of the Emergency. One of the historians selected to meet Chin Peng had been my University of London supervisor, AJ Stockwell — and he had taken me along to meet the man. Shortly afterward, I penned a report of the meeting with Chin Peng and sent it to my superiors back in Singapore.

S R Nathan's Probing Questions

When I next got back home, I was called up for a meeting with S R Nathan. Mr Nathan — 'S R' to those who knew him best — was not exactly a stranger to me. He and my late father had been colleagues in the civil service, and S R had known me since I was a child. The meeting I recall was, though cordial, very serious in tone. S R's background in external intelligence came across strongly as I was asked many questions about my meeting with Chin Peng.

One detail I will never forget is when S R showed me the report I had written and circled in red one portion: that Chin Peng had intimated during the June 1998 London meeting that the 1997/1998 Asian financial crisis had possibly created inclement domestic socioeconomic and political conditions that the CPM could exploit.

S R shared with me his assessment that this seemingly off-hand remark proved that the Communists had not changed. Eight years after the historic Haadyai peace accords that formally ended hostilities between the CPM and the Malaysian government, they were still seeking to upset the apple cart if the opportunity presented itself.

The Cold War's Impact

S R's comment to me revealed how much his professional life had been shaped by the Cold War — the nearly five-decade long ideological conflict between the US-led

Western democratic capitalist bloc and the Communist bloc led by the Soviet Union and China. The Cold War's legacy in Europe had been a divided continent paradoxically stabilised by the threat of mutual assured destruction via nuclear weapons.

In East Asia on the other hand, the Cold War had witnessed several 'hot' proxy wars in Korea in the 1950s, as well as Vietnam in the 1960s to 1970s. The CPM's jungle war in the 1950s against the British colonial and later independent Malayan governments was very much part of the wider Cold War fabric, as was its campaign — from the mid-1950s till the early 1960s — of urban subversion in Singapore, where it penetrated the deeply anticolonial Chinese-educated student and working classes.

S R, like the first generation PAP leaders led by Lee Kuan Yew, was very much immersed in this turbulent milieu. For them, their formative historical experiences had been dominated by what had seemed to them a long twilight struggle against a stubbornly resilient, determined, constantly shape-shifting foe. At one stage, the CPM was waging an armed insurgency in the Malayan jungle and later, it was infiltrating left-wing political parties, as well as student and labour unions, and rural associations in Singapore itself.

The Communists moreover appeared patient and not above staging comebacks: against the backdrop of the Cultural Revolution in China in the mid-1960s and Mao Zedong's grand design to exploit the upheavals in Southeast Asia, such as *Konfrontasi*, and the growing US military intervention in Vietnam, the CPM re-launched the armed struggle against Malaysia and Singapore in 1969.

CPM's Urban Terrorism

By the 1970s, Kuala Lumpur and Singapore had to contend with CPM-inspired low-intensity urban terrorism, as well as a concerted radio propaganda campaign spearheaded by the notorious Voice of Malayan Revolution (VMR) radio station, led by English-educated CPM cadres operating from Chinese territory till the early 1980s. In this connection, S R once remarked to me how he had marvelled at the ability of CPM propaganda like VMR to address extremely mundane issues — such as how women could cope with the inconveniences arising from their monthly periods! To him, this was proof of the CPM's determination to go to any lengths to subvert Malaysia and Singapore, and establish its Communist Republic.

Faced with this threat, S R — like his first generation peers — developed an equally dogged determination to ensure that the Communists would be crushed. S R was thus one of the last first-generation, staunchly anti-Communist Cold Warriors. He reminds one of the late great Malaysian Psychological Warfare expert, C C Too, who like S R, never trusted the Communists.

Too warned Malaysian leaders not to be complacent — even after the end of the Cold War, and the new Chinese leader Deng Xiaoping's decision to cut support for 'fraternal' Communist Parties in the region had forced

Chin Peng to the negotiating table by the end of the 1980s.

S R Nathan the Man

S R Nathan the Cold Warrior was, as it turned out, just one attribute — if an important one — of the man. He was to prove himself, in Lee Kuan Yew's words, the "indispensable man for all seasons", displaying great political acumen in a range of duties from running intelligence and security services and foreign ministry to newspapers and think tanks — as well as representing Singapore in key diplomatic assignments.

However, he could be thoroughly down-to-earth too. About two years ago, my god-daughter asked me if he could speak at a secondary school event for ASEAN students. I knew by then that although he had relinquished the presidency, he was not in the best of health. I was thus uncertain if I should even raise the subject. I did so gingerly one day and to my surprise, he indicated he would be happy to do so.

He kept his word as well, addressing the multinational student audience at my god-daughter's school, gamely answering their questions, and posing for numerous photographs with them, demonstrating once again the human touch many have remarked upon. This was a man who effortlessly operated at the level of heads of state as well as that of the ordinary man on the street. He modelled for me what a full and meaningful life looks like.

In Anfield stadium, home of Liverpool Football Club in England, there is a statue of Bill Shankly, the legendary Scot manager of that famous club. At the base of the statue, there is a simple epitaph: "He made the people happy." S R Nathan was a man of many profound achievements. I suspect, however, that many Singaporeans would agree that among his greatest was surely that, in his own inimitable way, he made the people happy.

Associate Professor Kumar Ramakrishna is the Head of Policy Studies and Coordinator of National Security Studies Programme at the S. Rajaratnam School of International Studies. Associate Professor Kumar was recruited by Mr Nathan to join the Institute of Defence and Strategic Studies in 1999 while completing his doctoral studies in London.

S R Nathan and the Institute of Defence and Strategic Studies (IDSS): The Formative Years

Ang Cheng Guan

Mr S R Nathan had recounted the formative years (1996–1999) of the Institute of Defence and Strategic Studies (IDSS) in Chapter 9 of his autobiography *An Unexpected Journey: Path to the Presidency*, published in 2011. The setting up of the Institute with a unique dual think-tank and teaching role was his last assignment before he was called upon to run for the Elected Presidency, which of course he did not expect in 1996, when he returned from Washington, DC after completing his term as Singapore's Ambassador to the United States. He was already 72 years of age when he took on the responsibility to establish the IDSS, which he initially felt that he might not be, in his own words, "well-qualified" to do. Mr S R Nathan proved to be more than capable. By the time, he left IDSS to become the sixth President of Singapore, IDSS, despite being the youngest think tank in the region then, has become considerably well-known in the think tank community. Had he not been asked to run for the Presidency in 1999, I would think that he would have retired as Ambassador-at Large, and Director of IDSS.

I had the privilege of working for Mr S R Nathan during those three years when he was Director of IDSS, and had a first-hand view of how he set up the think tank-cum-teaching institute from scratch. His passing brings back memories of those years. How I came to join IDSS as a fresh PhD had been mentioned in his memoir and there is no need to repeat it here. I did not have a job title when he took me on in 1996. My job scope was simply to help him set up the Institute, and in that capacity, I got to know Mr Nathan as a person, as a boss, and a mentor.

As mentioned above, IDSS had a dual mission as both a think tank and a teaching institute. Mr Nathan went about developing both wings very carefully and methodically. Despite his vast experience and seniority, he was very humble and very cognizant of his strengths and limitations, always ready to learn and engage others who know more than him. He was naturally very much more familiar with the think tank side of IDSS, given his years of experience in defence and foreign affairs. Even then, one of the first things he did was to visit some of the very established think tanks in the neighbourhood, the UK and the United States, to introduce IDSS, and to learn how they function. One of the major initiatives of Mr Nathan was the invitation of the key Indonesian political personalities who had presidential aspirations in the immediate post-Suharto period to IDSS, to share their views and visions for both Indonesia and the region. This initiative immediately enhanced the profile of IDSS. Few know that Mr Nathan planted the idea of the annual forum of defence ministers known as the 'Shangri-La Dialogue'. IDSS was still very much in its infancy with a skeleton staff, and lacked an international reputation to be able to pull off such a high-level event. It was thus left to the IISS (London) to organise it with support from IDSS. Those were the days when we still worked a half-day on Saturdays, and Mr Nathan would occasionally bring his grandchildren Monisha and Kiron to help us do photocopying and stapling. IDSS was however able to bring together a number of policy advisers and opinion makers from the region and beyond for a closed-door roundtable to discuss regional security issues. Mr Nathan also conceived the idea of the 'Summer Camp' for military officers (now known as APPSMO), which I have recounted in *The APPSMO Advantage*.

Mr Nathan was, as he acknowledged, less familiar with academia. However, he paid equal attention to the teaching function of IDSS. He engaged the world renowned Professor of Strategic Studies, Professor (and now Sir) Lawrence Freedman, then based at King's College London, as the consultant for the teaching programme which quickly gave it the credibility it needed. Mr Nathan would remind me that while we want to grow the teaching programme and attract more students, IDSS must be careful not to become a degree mill.

He also recruited Harvard-trained Associate Professor Khong Yuen Foong, then based at Nuffield College,

Oxford University, as his deputy Director in IDSS, to fill the gap which he knew he lacked — the academic community network. Khong joined IDSS in 1998 and, through him, many prominent Strategic Studies and International Relations scholars visited IDSS to give lectures as well as to teach, which helped to raise the profile of IDSS as an academic institution as well.

Mr Nathan not only thought of the short term, although given his age, I believe he wanted to accomplish his assignment as fast as he could. With one eye on quickly making IDSS a recognised name in the think tank/academic community, his other eye was trained on the long-term development and sustainability of the Institute. Professor Joseph Liow, the current Dean, is an example of the outcome of Mr Nathan's long-term vision of ensuring that the Institute would have its own in-house specialists. In those early days, our principal in-house expert was Mr Nathan himself, and everyone, from far and near, wanted to meet and discuss regional affairs with him. I benefitted very much from just sitting in in his meetings and discussions.

Ambassador Ong Keng Yong, in his eulogy, spoke of how Mr Nathan's "diplomatic skills and energy level" left him "panting for breath very often". Indeed, Mr Nathan was really full of energy even in his 70s. When I travelled with him, his days would be packed with meetings, and at breakfast the very next morning, he would be there before me with the summary of the discussions of the previous day. Mr Nathan's reputation as a tough boss was legendary. I recall a senior civil servant who once asked me with a slight smile, how it was like working for Mr Nathan. I think he must have mellowed with age. He never said a harsh word to me, but I really had to be on my toes most of the time. Mr Nathan was concurrently Ambassador-at-Large, and he had another office in the Ministry of Foreign Affairs which was then located at Raffles City. I could always expect a call from him on his mobile phone after he left IDSS for MFA or vice versa, with instructions on one thing or another. He never stopped working even in the car. I would often be summoned to his MFA office as well. Mr Nathan certainly left a strong foundation for his successor to work on.

Work aside, Mr Nathan was very nurturing. He brought me along on a number of his visits to think tanks overseas, and also sent me to attend many conferences and workshops to learn about international relations and security issues. He would instruct me to find out how the think tanks operate and to invite them to establish ties with IDSS. I recall spending two weeks at RAND at Santa Monica, USA in 1997. RAND was then perhaps the only think tank in the world that had a teaching function, although it was only for the PhD programme. RSIS now also has a small PhD programme.

I also remember fondly the many times Mr Nathan would ask me out for lunch, and we would go to a nearby hawker or food centre near NTU. Occasionally, we would travel further, for example, he brought me to Komala Vilas in Little India. He enjoyed local food especially *mee rebus*. The last lunch I had with him before he became President was at the NUS Guild House, where we were given an extra serving of *mee rebus* because the restaurant staff recognised him. He said he would not be able to eat out so easily in future.

Associate Professor Ang Cheng Guan *is the Head of Graduate Studies at the S. Rajaratnam School of International Studies. Associate Professor Ang previously worked with Mr S R Nathan at the Institute of Defence and Strategic Studies.*

Nurturing a New Generation of Scholars

Joseph C Y Liow, Bernard Loo and Bhubhindar Singh

As the founding Director of the Institute of Defence and Strategic Studies (IDSS), S R Nathan was tasked to build a think tank from scratch, with minimal resources and hardly any staff. With commitment, foresight, and energy that characterised the leaders of his generation, S R Nathan would prove more than up to the task. From day one, he set about his assignment with a sense of purpose but also humility. In those early years, he spent much time travelling the world, seeking meetings with the leaders of various think tanks and institutes of strategic studies, with the intention to learn from them the trade of 'think-tanking' and policy and academic research. Neither did the fact that IDSS in those early days was operating with a skeleton staff stop him from hosting major events. Barely a year into its existence, the tiny IDSS, with a staff strength of barely a dozen from the director to the driver, hosted its first ever distinguished public lecture in 1997, when US Secretary of Defense William Cohen spoke to an audience of more than 400.

His countless achievements during the course of a distinguished career aside, one of the most lasting — and crucial — aspects of S R Nathan's contribution in service of Singapore was his absolute commitment to grooming the younger generations. This was clearly evident in the role he played in the defence and foreign ministries. It was no less evident when he helmed IDSS.

At IDSS, S R Nathan paid considerable attention to the development of young scholars and researchers. During his three years as Director, he employed a large number of researchers as research assistants and associate research fellows (ARF). Research assistants possessed only a basic degree, while ARFs were Master degree-holders. To be sure, given the need to staff the institute and the dearth of available senior specialists, S R Nathan was probably compelled at least in part to look to younger, less experienced researchers. However, to us, there was more than an element of long-term planning and foresight involved. This would become clear in the support, attention, and leeway that he gave us, the younger scholars. Foremost in his mind, even in those early years, was the need to lay a firm foundation for the future of IDSS.

For the junior researchers, S R Nathan proved to be the perfect mentor and boss. He gave us time and space to grow into our jobs, and was always prepared to consider our perspectives and analyses of regional developments, no matter how naïve and shallow our views sometimes appeared. All this was done in the spirit of the IDSS motto that he coined: "Ponder the

Improbable". Even when he saw a need to correct us in order to ensure our feet were firmly planted on the ground, he would do so in a nurturing way. Indeed, although we had all by then heard of his reputation as a tough but caring boss, in the two to three years we worked for him, we experienced far more care than we did toughness. Perhaps he had mellowed with age. Whatever the case may be, the fact was that this created a positive environment for us to develop intellectually.

There were two qualities of his leadership that we all found impressive. First, S R Nathan had a clear vision for the institution, and idea of the areas of research expertise he required for the fledgling IDSS. He identified these areas based on Singapore's national interests and his vast knowledge accumulated from his extensive experience at the forefront of Singapore's defence and diplomacy. These areas included expertise in Indonesia, Malaysia, China, Japan, and the United States. Not surprisingly, the first four researchers he hired were 'assigned' to focus on Indonesia, Malaysia, China, and Japan. To enhance our knowledge, S R Nathan sent us for intensive language training, and encouraged us to make regular visits to the respective countries in order to deepen our understanding of local dynamics and strengthen our networks. Put differently, he set us on the path of becoming serious country, if not area, specialists. Apart from research into the foreign policies and domestic politics of key regional states, S R Nathan also envisaged IDSS playing a crucial role in defence education. To fulfil this mission, he brought in young scholars prepared to pursue careers in military and strategic studies.

To S R Nathan, it was important that RSIS had a Singaporean core. Most of us in the 'first generation' at IDSS were Singaporeans. A firm believer in education and training, S R Nathan persuaded the agencies that supported IDSS in those early years to provide funding for scholarships for young IDSS researchers to pursue their PhDs. Several of us were very fortunate to have been beneficiaries of this support. Two decades later, not a few of the young scholars that S R Nathan recruited in those early years have become internationally-recognised experts in their own right.

Professor Joseph Liow, the current dean of RSIS, began life as a Malaysianist under the tutorship of S R Nathan. Associate Professor Bhubhindar Singh was encouraged to pursue an incipient interest in Japan, and today, is recognised as an authority in Japanese foreign policy. Associate Professor Bernard Loo has made significant contributions to military education in Singapore after graduating from the University of Aberystwyth with a PhD funded by an IDSS scholarship. We are proud to report that all of us have published notable scholarly and policy-relevant research on the countries and areas S R Nathan tasked us to study many years ago, and in doing so, we have hopefully played a small part contributing to the growth of IDSS and RSIS, as S R Nathan envisaged.

There is a Chinese saying, 飲水思源 (yǐn shuǐ sī yuán), that teaches one not to forget the source of the water which one drinks. For the young scholars of IDSS who had the privilege of working for S R Nathan, we have been, and will always be, grateful for the faith and trust he placed in us by investing in our development, providing us opportunities, and supporting us every step of the way. We all are, and always will be, in his debt.

Jauh sungguh pergi mandi	Far indeed we travel to bathe;
Maksud hati hendak bertapa	The intent was to meditate;
Berat sungguh menanggung budi	Heavy indeed is the burden of debt
Seribu tahun tak boleh lupa.	It cannot be forgotten for a thousand years.

Professor Joseph CY Liow *is Dean of the S. Rajaratnam School of International Studies,* **Associate Professor Bernard Loo** *is the Coordinator of the Master of Science (Strategic Studies) degree programme at the S. Rajaratnam School of International Studies (RSIS), and* **Associate Professor Bhubhindar Singh** *is the Coordinator of the Regional Security Architecture Programme at the S. Rajaratnam School of International Studies. All three authors previously worked with Mr S R Nathan at the Institute of Defence and Strategic Studies.*

Appendices

1. Testimonial Letter from Miss Jean M Robertson, Senior Lecturer, University of Malaya, 1955

2. Citation for the Conferment of Fellow of the Singapore Association of Social Workers to Mr S R Nathan by Associate Professor Ann Wee, 2008

3. Citation for the Honorary Degree of Doctor of Letters by the Public Orator, Professor Bertil Andersson, President, Nanyang Technological University, 6 December 2011

4. Speech by Mr S R Nathan Director, Institute of Defence and Strategic Studies at the Inauguration Ceremony, 1996

1. **Testimonial Letter from Miss Jean M Robertson, Senior Lecturer, University of Malaya, 1955**

University of Malaya
Department of Social Studies

Cluny Road, Singapore

30 December 1955

Mr J C Litton
Principal Assistant Director
Social Welfare Department
Ministry of Labour and Welfare
Havelock Road
Singapore

Dear Mr Litton,

You asked me a short time ago whether I could make any suggestions of persons to be included in a delegation from Singapore to the International Conference on Social Work to be held in Munich next year.

In my experience, delegations from the various countries to this conference are generally composed very largely of professionally qualified social workers of some standing in their own country, together occasionally with other persons particularly concerned with the administration of social services, either statutory or voluntary, and very often a member of the teaching staff of a University Department of Social Studies.

Of course the delegations vary, but that is the usual pattern in delegations from such countries as the UK, Australia, Canada, and so on. Also, any other persons who are interested in social work may attend the conference, even though they are not included as members of a delegation.

I should like to see included in the Singapore delegation at least one of the younger Asian professionally qualified social workers who is likely to make a contribution to social work in this country in the future, and I have one person in mind whom I think would be particularly suitable.

He is Mr S R Nathan, who took his diploma in Social Studies in this University in 1954, gaining a Distinction. He is at present studying for an external degree of London University. He was, without doubt, the best student we have had both on the practical and theoretical sides, and is a person for whom I have a very high regard. He is aged 31, is a person of maturity with some knowledge before entering the course of trade union organisation, and with a very considerable interest in the social problems of industry. He was awarded the

Shell Bursary for a student intending to do social work in industry or commerce.

Since qualifying, he has been working as a social worker with the Medical Department, Singapore, particularly concerned in developing work in the rural areas, but is shortly to take up an appointment as Assistant Seamen's Welfare Officer in the Ministry of Commerce and Industry. He is a person who is held in high regard wherever he goes, and was indeed approached by the Government to take the post in Seamen's Welfare, on which subject he had already written a very good thesis; and other employers, such as the City Council and the Social Welfare Department, Federation of Malaya, have also been anxious to secure his services.

He is tolerant and moderate in outlook, with a receptive mind. His knowledge and interests are wide, and he is, I think, very well able to profit by attendance at the International Conference of Social Work, and would be able to bring back a good deal of what he had learned, to pass on to other people here. He has not been overseas before, and this would give him a valuable experience.

He is at present the Secretary of the pro tem committee which is planning the setting up of an association of professional social workers in Singapore, and I think it is very likely that he may be elected the Chairman of the body when it is officially formed.

He has a quick and lively mind, is prepared to contribute to discussions, and has a good knowledge of social problems in Singapore, and a particular interest in the human problems of industry, as well as knowledge from observation of the effects of family life of industrialisation such as we see in Singapore, which would be of particular relevance to the subject of the conference.

I feel that in every way he would be a good choice as a member of the delegation and I hope it may be possible to include him.

Yours sincerely,

Miss Jean M Robertson
Senior Lecturer

2. Citation for the Conferment of Fellow of the Singapore Association of Social Workers to Mr S R Nathan by Associate Professor Ann Wee, 2008

Mr President of the Singapore Association of Social Workers,

The President of the Republic of Singapore, Mr S R Nathan, stands before us as an outstandingly qualified and worthy candidate for the conferment of the honour of appointment, as Fellow of the Singapore Association of Social Workers.

Mr Nathan made his first steps into the category 'outstanding', while still a young man, as this narrative will soon illustrate. Following a hardworking and well-spent early youth, in 1952, Mr Nathan became a member of the first cohort to take the Diploma in Social Studies course, at the then University of Malaya. Within the Diploma examination regulations, statutory provision had been made only for Pass or Fail status. In the final year of this first cohort, examiners noted that one student was so far ahead of what was on the whole a good class, that this limited categorisation of results was grossly inequitable. In order to right this injustice, the University did what universities and all statutory bodies are most loath to do, and indeed are only very rarely moved to do — it added a *retrospective* clause to the regulations, so that in 1954, Mr Nathan's outstanding final examination performance could be recorded as Pass with Distinction.

Mr Nathan's work as a student was marked by another, and even more outstanding achievement. He is most certainly unique in local university records, in that his research findings as a student, (and a student below post-graduate level at that), led to the setting up from scratch of a new and pioneering government department. Mr Nathan's final year dissertation, revealed that lodging housekeepers in the dock area, were running a system which amounted to debt enslavement, of Asian merchant seaman awaiting their next shipboard employment.

Mr Nathan's research findings were drawn to the attention of the then Chief Minister, whose government forthwith set up the Asian Seaman's Registry, and in 1956, Mr Nathan was appointed as the first Asian Seaman's Welfare Officer.

Prior to this appointment, and following graduation, Mr Nathan had been working in Tan Tock Seng Hospital. This being the first occasion ever, that a man had filled a Singapore medical social work post, the Hospital took time to make adjustments. For a while, Mr Nathan manfully performed his duties with fine professionalism, despite being based in an office bearing the door label 'Lady Almoner'.

Following some years in the position of Asian Seaman's Welfare Officer, and a four-year secondment as Director of the Labour Research Unit of NTUC, in1966, Mr Nathan was promoted to the Administrative Service. His postings included the Ministries of Defence, Foreign Affairs and Home Affairs. In both the latter two Ministries, he held the position of Permanent Secretary.

In 1982, Mr Nathan was appointed Executive Chairman of The Straits Times. In this position, he exercised leadership with his usual distinction, and enjoyed good relationships with, and the confidence of the varied and sometimes maverick personalities who always go to the making up of a lively journalist team.

In 1988, Mr Nathan began a new career as a diplomat, first as our High Commissioner to Malaysia, and then from 1990 to 1996, he served as Singapore's Ambassador to the United States, possibly the most senior posting in our diplomatic service. Mr Nathan's time in Washington covered a most difficult period in Singapore–USA relations, namely what has come to be referred to as the Michael Fay affair. Singapore's firm handling of the vandalism committed by an 18-year-old American citizen, raised such outcry in the United States, that it looked for some time as if our American friends were about to send a gunboat up the Singapore river. Mr Nathan's diplomatic skills played no small part in his country's dealing with this difficult interlude in our foreign relations.

On a lighter note, it was during Mr Nathan's time in Washington, that the embassy residence there was purchased. Our present ambassador has expressed appreciation that this was so, and that subsequent Singapore representatives can thereby benefit from the good sense and impeccable good taste of then Ambassador and Mrs Nathan.

In 1996, when at age 74, most Singaporeans would have been long allowed to retire, Mr Nathan was much too valuable to be spared, and he graciously agreed in the three years prior to his present high office, to head the Institute of Defence and Strategic Studies, at Nanyang Technological University.

Alongside this magnificent life record of service to the public sector, Mr Nathan also gave significantly in voluntary work. For many years, he served as Honorary Secretary to the then Singapore Council of Social Service. Those who had the honour to serve on the Council at that time, can vouch for the dedication and energy Mr Nathan brought to that role, despite the pressures of his demanding professional career. Mr Nathan has also served as Chair of the Hindu Endowments Board, and was a founder member of the Singapore Indian Development Association, or SINDA.

Of Mr Nathan's appointment as our President of the Republic and the high esteem in which he has been held in this office, the facts are too well known to permit recounting on this occasion. His dignity and wisdom have enhanced Singapore's international standing, his humanity and kindness have touched the hearts of Singaporeans of all races and creeds.

However, Mr President, over and above all Mr Nathan's other and many outstanding and matchless life achievements, there is one awesome interlude in his career, which even if standing alone qualifies him for the most high honour which it is within the clauses of our constitution to award. Older members of our profession will never forget his role in the tense and terrible days in early 1974, that is remembered as the 'Laju incident'.

A group of Japanese and Palestinian terrorists had managed to enter Singapore waters, with the specific intention of blowing up the major oil installations on the island, Pulau Bukum. Our intelligence services were able to frustrate any such dreadful event, but not before the group had hijacked the ferry servicing Pulau Bukum, the Laju, and taking the Singaporean crew members as hostages.

Rarely have Singaporeans lived through such days of tension and anxiety, as was the case while delicate negotiations ensued, to ensure the lives and safety of that citizen crew. Eventually a compromise was reached: the terrorists would lay down their arms, in return for safe passage by air, to a destination in Kuwait, but only if accompanied by 13 senior Singapore government officials, as guarantors. Of this virtually hostage contingent, Mr Nathan, who had played a leadership role in the negotiations, agreed to act as *chef de mission*.

The contingent returned safely to a tumultuous welcome, and were greeted by the press on the tarmac. "Mr Nathan", asked one reporter, "throughout this dreadful time, you always seemed so calm and confident. How did you manage this?" In what must be one of our professions proudest moments, Mr Nathan replied without hesitation: "because I am a trained social worker".

Associate Professor Ann Wee
Honorary Member SASW

3. **Citation for the Honorary Degree of Doctor of Letters by the Public Orator, Professor Bertil Andersson, President, Nanyang Technological University, 6 December 2011**

May I invite Mr S R Nathan to rise to acknowledge the citation and the acclaim of this Conferment, please.

Sellapan Ramanathan, more widely known as S R Nathan, rose from modest beginnings to become the sixth President of the Republic of Singapore. Mr Nathan's formal education was disrupted by family circumstances and the war years, but, with grit and determination, he would go on to complete his schooling through self-study and to graduate from the University of Malaya in 1954, with a Diploma in Social Studies with Distinction. His career in the Singapore Civil Service began with medical social work in 1955. He then served in various government agencies and ministries, including the labour movement, and what would later become the Ministries of Foreign Affairs, Home Affairs, and Defence. For his distinguished services, he was awarded the Public Service Star in 1964, when he was serving as Director of the Labour Research Unit, and the Public Administration Medal (Silver) in 1967 shortly after he was transferred to the Ministry of Foreign Affairs.

When Mr Nathan was Director of MINDEF's Security and Intelligence Department, he demonstrated courage and leadership when he negotiated an end to the Laju hostage crisis of 1974, in the process of which he and a team of government officials bravely volunteered to take the place of several people who had been taken hostage by the Palestinian and Japanese Red Army terrorists. In 1974, Mr Nathan was awarded the Meritorious Service Medal.

Mr Nathan returned to the Ministry of Foreign Affairs in 1979, where he served as First Permanent Secretary until 1982. He then became Executive Chairman of The Straits Times Press, holding directorships in various companies and chairing the Hindu Endowments Board from 1983 to 1988. Mr Nathan was appointed Singapore's High Commissioner to Malaysia in 1988, and then Ambassador to the United States in 1990. On returning from the United States in 1996, Mr Nathan, then Ambassador-at-Large, was appointed founding Director of the Institute of Defence and Strategic Studies (IDSS), which was established on July 30, 1996 as an autonomous institute in NTU. IDSS was later renamed the S Rajaratnam School of International Studies (RSIS) on January 1, 2007.

The success of RSIS today owes much to Mr Nathan. As Director of IDSS, he laid strong foundations for his successors to build upon. Besides establishing IDSS as a professional graduate school of international affairs, he also insisted on research being policy-relevant. His exhortation to faculty and research staff to "Ponder the Improbable" was a timely encouragement in view of the terrorist attacks of September 11, 2001, which was closely followed by the SARS pandemic and its impact on global economies in 2003. His international outlook and his foreign policy background led to an emphasis on networking, which has contributed to knowledge sharing between RSIS and think tanks from all over the world, and to RSIS' standing as a critical node in the international network of think tanks and academic institutions dealing with strategic and security studies.

As we all know, there was yet another higher calling for Mr Nathan when he moved on from these sterling achievements in the public and diplomatic service to step forward to be elected as President of the Republic of Singapore in August 1999.

As President of Singapore, Mr Nathan also served as Chancellor of Nanyang Technological University. As Chancellor, Mr Nathan was closely associated with the development of the university and always had an intense interest in what was happening at NTU throughout his two terms. He played a key role in the recruitment of key personnel, establishment of major research institutes such as the Earth Observatory of Singapore and the Institute of Catastrophe Risk Management, and development of links with key institutions and personalities such as the former President of India, Dr Abdul Kalam.

Mr Nathan extended his strong support to the university's initiatives and student activities. He has always been very generous with his time for NTU, and made it a point to get to know the students and faculty well. As a most engaged President, he served as a wonderful role model for our graduates and inspired many with his dedication and integrity.

As Chancellor of NTU, Mr Nathan was the patron of various University fundraising efforts. He played an instrumental role in raising a record donation for the Lee Kong Chian School of Medicine and was involved in fundraising campaigns such as the NTU 21st Century Fund, the Wee Kim Wee School of Communication and Information's Wee Kim Wee Legacy Fund, and the RSIS Endowment Fund.

An honorary doctorate is one of higher education's most significant accolades. When a Doctor of Letters is conferred *honoris causa* ('for the sake of honour'), it acknowledges the pre-eminence of its recipient. In this instance, it recognises the distinguished and sustained achievements of a man spanning five and a half decades of public service; selfless commitment to the University and to the cause of higher learning; and steady contributions both to the Nation, to international relations and this University and its endeavours.

We recognise today an outstanding public career, through which the recipient has served Singapore and its academic system in particular with dedication and distinction. We also acknowledge his considerable support for NTU, which has enhanced the standing of the University at the local, regional and global levels. And indeed NTU is honoured that Mr Nathan will continue his close association with the University as Distinguished Senior Fellow of RSIS.

It is my privilege to present to you Mr S R Nathan, for the award of the degree of Doctor of Letters, *honoris causa*.

4. Speech by Mr S R Nathan
Director, Institute of Defence and Strategic Studies at the Inauguration Ceremony, 1996

Mr Deputy Prime Minister and Minister for Defence, Minister, Your Excellencies, Distinguished Guests, Ladies and Gentlemen.

On behalf of the Institute's Board of Governors, I would like, first of all to thank Deputy Prime Minister Dr Tony Tan Keng Yam for gracing this ceremony and inaugurating the Institute of Defence and Strategic Studies. Secondly, I would like to thank the Singapore Totalisator Board for their very generous donation towards the Institute's Endowment Fund, without which the inauguration today of this Institute would not have been possible.

As the Deputy Prime Minister has just said, the need for this Institute is obvious in today's fast changing strategic environment. With the end of the Cold War and widespread expectations of unlimited growth, the need for such an Institute may be lost on many. But we cannot afford to forget, as has happened elsewhere many times in the past, that none of us are invulnerable to the forces of change, especially in a fast-changing and unpredictable strategic environment. For us in

Singapore and the region, the implications are far more complex. They call for the shaping of new thinking and the discarding of misleading precepts and out dated assumptions.

If this Institute is to serve its purpose, it would be necessary first to develop, and in due time nurture, a core of knowledgeable scholars engaged in the continuous study of questions of strategic interest to Singapore and the region around us. They will also have to come up with definitive suggestions on how best to deal with a world, that hardly resembles, what we have all been familiar with, until recent times. For these are times when new strategies of regional security are also in the making.

It is the hope of the Board of Governors that the Institute will develop scholarship and expertise to seek answers, and develop persuasive tools, to address complex problems of diplomacy and security. For these will be so necessary for the continued preservation and promotion of our sovereignty and national integrity.

The task entrusted to the Institute is a professional challenge to all who will work in it. We will have to address fundamental and difficult questions, like what global and regional challenges that emerge from time to time could mean for Singapore, and the Southeast Asian region. It goes without saying that the Institute's contribution will also help understand how best to limit the risks of conflict, in an unpredictable world. I am confident that those who will work in this Institute will respond to this professional challenge with equal vigour and determination.

Lastly, I would like to thank the Nanyang Technological University Council and the Governing Board of the Institute for giving me the privilege to serve as the Institute's first Director.

List of Abbreviations

AAPSO	Afro-Asian Peoples' Solidarity Organisation
ABRI	Armed Forces of the Republic of Indonesia
AFP	Agence France-Presse
AP	The Associated Press
APPSMO	Asia Pacific Programme for Senior Military Officers
ARF	Associate Research Fellow
ASEAN	Association of Southeast Asian Nations
AUPE	Amalgamated Union of Public Employees
BBC	British Broadcasting Corporation
CHOGM	Commonwealth Heads of Government Meeting
CHOGRM	Commonwealth Heads of Government Regional Meeting
CPM	Communist Party of Malaya
CSCAP	Council for Security Cooperation in the Asia Pacific
D/R+E	Director of Regional and Economic Division
DCM	Deputy Chief of Mission
DPRK	Democratic People's Republic of Korea
EU	European Union
GATT	General Agreement on Tariffs and Trade

GTO	Government Team of Officials
HDB	Housing and Development Board
IDSA	Institute for Defence Studies and Analyses
IDSS	Institute of Defence and Strategic Studies
IISS	International Institute for Strategic Studies
IRO	Inter-Religious Organisation
ISEAS	Institute of Southeast Asian Studies
ISIS	Institute of Strategic and International Studies
IVCO	International Volunteer Cooperation Organisations
JAL	Japan Airlines
KL	Kuala Lumpur
KPNLF	Khmer People's National Liberation Front
LRU	Labour Research Unit
MFA	Ministry of Foreign Affairs
MHA	Ministry of Home Affairs
MINDEF	Ministry of Defence
NGO	Non-Governmental Organisation
NTU	Nanyang Technological University
NTUC	National Trades Union Congress
NUS	National University of Singapore
PAP	People's Action Party
PFLP	Popular Front for the Liberation of Palestine
PM	Prime Minister
PMO	Prime Minister's Office
PSC	Public Service Commission
PUB	Public Utilities Board
ROK	Republic of Korea

RSIS	S. Rajaratnam School of International Studies
SAF	Singapore Armed Forces
SATU	Singapore Association of Trade Unions
SGH	Singapore General Hospital
SIA	Singapore Airlines
SID	Security and Intelligence Division
SIF	Singapore International Foundation
SINDA	Singapore Indian Development Association
SIET	Singapore Indian Education Trust
SMU	Singapore Management University
SOS	Samaritans of Singapore
SPH	Singapore Press Holdings
ST	The Straits Times
SNUJ	Singapore National Union of Journalists
SWB	Seamen's Welfare Board
UK	United Kingdom
UM	University of Malaya
UN	United Nations
US/USA	United States of America
USTR	United States Trade Representative
VMR	Voice of Malayan Revolution
WTO	World Trade Organisation

References

Nathan, S R. 2011. *Winning Against The Odds: The Labour Research Unit in NTUC's Founding.* Singapore: Straits Times Press.

Nathan, S R. 2011. *An Unexpected Journey: Path to the Presidency.* Singapore: Editions Didier Millet.

Nathan, S R. 2013. *50 Stories from My Life.* Singapore: Editions Didier Millet.

Nathan, S R and Timothy Auger. 2015. *S R Nathan in Conversation with Timothy Auger.* Singapore: Editions Didier Millet.

www.ingramcontent.com/pod-product-compliance
Lightning Source LLC
Chambersburg PA
CBHW070308230426
43664CB00015B/2672